Rottweilers

TO

CORKY AND KELLY

ROTTWEILERS

AN OWNER'S COMPANION

Les Price

HOWELL BOOK HOUSE
New York

MAXWELL MACMILLAN CANADA
Toronto

MAXWELL MACMILLAN INTERNATIONAL
New York Oxford Singapore Sydney

First published in Great Britain in 1991 by
The Crowood Press Ltd

Howell Book House
Macmillan Publishing Company
866 Third Avenue
New York, NY 10022

Maxwell Macmillan Canada, Inc.
1200 Eglinton Avenue East, Suite 200
Don Mills, Ontario M3C 3N1

Macmillan Publishing Company is part of the Maxwell Communication Group of
Companies.

Library of Congress Cataloging-in-Publication Data

Price, Les.
    Rottweilers : an owner's companion/Les Price.
    p. cm
    Includes bibliographical references and index.
    ISBN 0-87605-297-9
    1. Rottweiler dog. I. Title.
SF429.R7P75 1991   91-11326
636.7'3--dc20   CIP

Macmillan books are available at special discounts for bulk purchases for sales
promotions, premiums, fund-raising, or educational use. For details, contact:

Special Sales Director
Macmillan Publishing Company
866 Third Avenue
New York, NY 10022

10 9 8 7 6 5 4

Typeset by DTS Photoset, Swindon.
Printed in Great Britain by Butler & Tanner Ltd, Frome.

Contents

Foreword

During the past years great changes have taken place in dogs: their health, care, breeding and training. Each individual aspect of dogdom has now become a complete science and discipline; indeed, as I pen this foreword, a working party comprising the leading authorities on all aspects of dogs are compiling a nationally recognizable qualification allied to the 'City and Guilds' degree. This will enable those eager and able to sit the relevant examination and thus qualify. Such qualifications will be recognized by the leading organizations within the world of dogs. In my opinion, this dog book will have its place on such a curriculum.

I welcome this book on two major counts: first, because it succeeds in what should be the aim of every author, that is to educate and entertain, and secondly because it has been written by very knowledgeable person who genuinely cares for his dogs, has bred a consistent type for many years and has put as much into the 'dog game' as he has taken out. One must appreciate that with the passing of time all things progress; what may have been of considerable interest to one generation may not be to the next. This book will, however, stand the test of time. In a few instances as might be expected, opinions differ on certain aspects. I leave it to the readers to draw their own conclusions intelligently.

May I finally express a wish that readers of this book will enjoy the text, perhaps learn, but most importantly debate and discuss it.

Terry McHaffie M.B.E.
Chief Training Officer, Royal Air Force Police Dog School

1

History of the Breed

The origin of the Rottweiler is obscured by the shadowy mists of history. However, most historians of the breed agree that the original blood was of Roman origin. The dog that accompanied the eleventh legion that was to conquer the area we now know as Rottweil in AD 74 would not be recognizable as the breed we know today.

To understand the Rottweiler lineage, it is necessary to go even further back in time. Long before Christ, dogs were used in the amphitheatres of Rome for fighting large cats (there were usually three dogs pitted against one lion). These dogs were known as Mollosus dogs. Dogs of this type were also used in the Asiatic wars against rival armies. So it can be understood that planned breeding is not a new idea. There are accounts of dogs of Mastiff type being exported from Britain to Rome through an agent known as the *Procurator Pugnacium* (provider of dogs). Only the best were good enough to grace the amphitheatres; a second class performance by man or beast was not tolerated and would probably lead to the inevitable 'thumbs down'. It is reasonable to assume, therefore, that there would be a residue of canine stock, who for one reason or another would be deemed unsuitable to die for the perverted pleasure of the gloating Roman nobility.

The dog which the eleventh legion would have taken with them would need some herding instinct, be fleet of foot and be powerful enough to guard the herd against wolf or bear. Colour or general type was not important. Driving the cattle that was to feed the troops through the Alps was a Herculean task and it would have been impossible without the dogs.

It is known that dogs of herding and hunting ability were already in north Switzerland and south Germany, an area once known as Helvetia. Best known is the marsh dog of the Swiss Lake people, which was capable of speed and also had a strong powerful jaw. Also, domestication of dogs and cattle had been undertaken some twelve hundred years ago in southern Europe by Azilian hunters who had used dogs to corner their prey. They were the first known tamers of animals.

7

Assyrians going to the Hunt.

Elika v Barrenstein BH. AD. Europajugendsieger 1986, owned by the author and his wife.

The dogs that came with the Romans probably mated with the indigenous population, helping to form many of the breeds we know today. In fact, the indigenous population probably had more influence than most historians believe. The Rottweiler is almost more of a Swiss-type dog than a German one. By this I mean, in Switzerland the Rottweiler has many close cousins, including the Bernese Mountain Dog, Appenzeller and Entlebuch. The Entlebuch is also docked and resembles the Rottweiler to such a degree that it is easy to believe in a common ancestry.

The Rottweiler originates from a town of the same name, Rottweil, known as Arae Flaviae by the Romans. It was an important administration and social centre and had been populated at least two thousand years BC. With the coming of the Romans, the town was developed and transformed. The Orphic mosaic found in Rottweil probably enhanced the house of a wealthy Roman. The Bath House, also discovered in the town, tells us how important a site this was. Building continued and the town was upgraded to a fortified villa. The most important buildings would have had red hand-made tiles on the roof and for this reason, the

9

region became known as Rottwil (red villa). This name was changed over a period of time to the name we know today, Rottweil. Between AD 250 and 260, the town was conquered by Suebi and Alemanni tribes who slaughtered the Roman habitation. One can only guess what became of the dogs of the town, for they were usually trained to guard their master's property to the death. Needless to say, some did survive and prosper.

By the Middle Ages, the town had become fortified and a royal court of justice, with jurisdiction over a wide area. It is the cattle dealers and butchers of the town who are of most interest to us, for it was they who took the dog of Rottweil and turned him to their use with great effect. Long drives were undertaken from town to town, even country to country. Over a period of time, the dog was moulded to his master's needs, calling on all the virtues of his ancestors: herding ability, speed, guarding ability, strength and power, but most of all, intelligence.

Two types began to emerge: a large ponderous type, used in a draft capacity, for instance, for pulling the butchers' carts full of meat; secondly, a smaller, more agile type, used mainly for herding. The latter is the type nearest to what we know today. Although very large dogs can still be found, they do not excel in the show ring or in the trials arenas.

It was because of this close association with the butchers and cattle drovers, that the Rottweiler was to become known as the *metzgerhunt,* or butcher's dog. One story is told of drovers who, at the end of a long drive, having sold their cattle, would go to the *beerkeller* to celebrate, but before they did, they would tie the money from the sale around the dog's neck, secure in the knowledge that no matter how drunk they became, their money would be safe until the morning! These were good times for the intrepid forefathers of our breed. However, it was not to last.

Two things caused a gradual decline in the number of Rottweilers. Firstly, donkeys began to be used in the draft capacity, which was not too serious a blow, but the advent of the train almost doomed the breed to extinction. Cattle were no longer taken on long drives, but were delivered by rail and cattle drives were then made illegal. This was the most important feature of the breed's decline from grace, since it was bred solely for work. When that work is taken away, the dog becomes a luxury and one which the simple people of that time could not afford. At the turn of the century, things looked very bleak for the Rottweiler. It is recorded that, at this time, only one bitch was resident in her home town.

Blanka v Eppendorfer-Baum, SchH III Sieger in 1954. Owned by
M Bruns.

In 1905, something happened; a silver lining on the cloud of doom. The Rottweiler was recognized as a police dog, and though it came fourth behind three other breeds, it was a start, a start to a new career and one the breed took to with relish. Once new people had become interested, other people followed and new uses were found for the breed. Used as tracking dogs and guide dogs for the blind, the Rottweiler's versatility and willingness to please his master once again came to his rescue.

After the Second World War, the showing of dogs became more and more popular and the acquisition of a new breed to exploit, or make one's name with, was the order of the day. In countries outside Germany, the discovery of a very old 'new' breed was therefore irresistible. During the 1960s, 1970s and 1980s, we have seen the exploitation of the breed lead to its streaking into the top ten of the most popular dogs in countries with active show circuits. This popularity has not been all to the good, but having said that, the Rottweiler has now made friends who are concerned with his welfare. It is hoped all will not be lost with this giant swing of the pendulum.

Fortunately, the breed had clear guidelines on which to develop

11

drawn up by the breed clubs in Germany. The first club of this type was the International Rottweiler and Leonberger Club. This was a short-lived club, but important if only for the fact that it drew up the first Breed Standard in 1901. Very little information on this club is available, but apparently it was first started in 1899. Incidentally, the first report of a Rottweiler being shown at an official dog show was at Heilbronn in 1882.

On 11 January 1907, the German Rottweiler Club was formed, DRK. Albert Graf, one of the founders, is generally recognized as being the first breeder of the type we would know today. As with many clubs, there were disagreements, one of which led to one of the members being dismissed. This former member then led the formation of a new club known as the Southern German Rottweiler Club. It was also very short-lived. Former members therefore joined a third club, the International Rottweiler Club (IRK).

The Breed Standards of both clubs were very similar, the major difference being personal conflict, so it was a happy conclusion when, in 1921, both sides merged and formed the Allgemeiner Deutscher Rottweiler Klub (ADRK).

The rise of the ADRK was rapid, with all shades of Rottweiler interest coming under its umbrella. With its motto 'Rottweiler breeding is working dog breeding', it has put together a unique package where no dog can become a show champion without first having working qualifications.

Working, therefore, comes first, although great strides forward have been made in conformation or beauty points, but at a very controlled level. Head shape was the first improvement. This was achieved by three potent sires. Close attention was paid to their offspring. Some well-known producers were Lord von der Teck, Arco Torfwerk and Hackel v Kohlerwald.

It was however in the late 1950s that a dog arrived who embodied everything that was thought to be correct, a living blueprint for further development. He was Int. Ch. and Triple Bundessieger, Harras v Sofienbusch, who was to become an American import, also gaining an American title. It is his type that has been projected as desirable up to the present time, although I feel that recently, Rottweilers in Germany have become slightly lighter in build and longer in the loin, a very workmanlike animal, designed for Schutzhund work. Where this racey type and this small but workable type will lead, I do not know. What we do know is that ADRK will keep a close eye on all matters concerning the breed.

Liesel v Hegnenbacher Landl, SchH I. AD. Owned by Herr Wolfgang Gaa.

Falko v Gruntenblick, SchH III IPO 3 FH. AD. Owned by Herr Wolfgang Gaa.

The Rottweiler in Great Britain

The first registrations in the UK took place in 1936, when the late Mrs Thelma Gray of the Rozavel Kennels imported two bitches from Germany, Diana v Analienburg and Enne v Psalvgau. Enne was imported in-whelp to the Welt Sieger (World Champion) Ido v Kohlerwald SchH.II. Enne was described as an excellent bitch bodywise but her head was not her fortune. She was sold to Mrs Paton and the litter was born in quarantine, but, as with so many litters in those days, distemper took a heavy toll.

All the puppies except one died. This bitch was called Anna v Rozavel. Anna was to become a very good working dog, qualifying CDex and winning good show placements including Best of Breed at Crufts in 1939.

When the war broke out, Anna was commissioned into the Army, where she did her service for her newly adopted country. Obviously, at the end of her service, she was too old for breeding and stayed with her handler until she died at the age of sixteen. Anna was a fine representative of the breed, possibly a little large in the ear, but excellent in head type, body and limbs.

Mrs Gray made further imports, including Arnolf v d Eichner Ruine and Asta v Norden, who were half-brother and -sister. But the finest import Mrs Gray made was the German bitch Int. Ch. Vefa v Kohlerwald. This bitch was also mated before she came into quarantine in this country, where she produced a large litter of ten. Again, disaster struck because all ten puppies died.

In 1938, two other dogs were brought over, Arbo v Gaisburg, who was imported by Mrs Simmons, a keen obedience worker and show goer; and Benno v Kohlerwald by Miss Homan. This dog was also taken into the Armed Forces, thus effectively ruining any chance of the breed making any progress in this country at that time.

The war years must have been really frustrating for the early Rottweiler enthusiasts. Mrs Gray's home was in fact requisitioned by the Army. She sent a few dogs to Ireland and, after the war, attempts to track them down only resulted in letters being sent back marked 'gone away'.

The second attempt at getting Rottweilers off the ground in the UK was not until 1953. Captain Frederick Roy-Smith was serving in Germany in the Royal Army Veterinary Corps and had seen Rottweilers who had impressed him greatly, especially with their working ability. Captain Roy-Smith brought back a breeding pair: the dog was Ajax v

Suhrenkamp and the bitch, Berny v Weyher. It is fortunate for the further success of the breed that the liaison between these two animals did not produce fruit, except on one occasion, since the bitch was in fact a long coat, and thus unable to be registered with the ADRK. Berny was destroyed in 1956, after six attempted matings, which produced a total of four puppies, of which only one survived. The Germans perhaps thought it was a huge joke to sell a long-coated bitch to someone who was to try to re-establish the breed in another country. I find this attitude hard to understand but it still prevails today.

The mortality rate of puppies at that time was incredible. It seemed that mortalities were the norm and survivals were very rare.

A second bitch was acquired by Captain Roy-Smith, Lotte v Osterburg, who was a much better breeding prospect and foundation for the breed in this country. She was mated to Ajax and produced two litters, the first one, in 1958, contained five dogs, four of which apparently went to India and Pakistan, for reasons which seem to be obscure. The only dog that remained in this country was Rintelna The Bombadier, who was bought by Mary MacPhail. He was to become the sire of the first British champion.

Rudi Eulenspiegel of Mallion, owned by Mrs Chadwick.

W. T. Ch. Bruin of Mallion, owned by Mrs Maud Wait.

Meanwhile, Mrs Joanne Chadwick of the Mallion Kennel was importing dogs from the Eulenspiegel Kennel in Germany. This kennel was owned and run by the famed German breeder Frau Marion Bruns. The first dogs to arrive on these shores from these kennels were a breeding pair: Rudi Eulenspiegel of Mallion and Quinta Eulenspiegel of Mallion. It is my belief that the Mallion lines do not receive the credit they deserve. Not only were they prolific breeding stock, but some very useful dogs were to appear from their matings. Best known of these was Bruin of Mallion, who belonged to Mrs Maud Wait of the Lenlee prefix. Bruin was to become the first Rottweiler to gain the title 'Champion' in the Working Trials arena. He gained the title of CDex/TDex. Against better-known breeds, this was a tremendous achievement.

Eric of Mallion was the first champion to be born in this country, but not the first to gain this title because he did not actually become a champion until he was seven years old. He was owned by Mrs Cook. Abelard of Mallion was the first Rottweiler to be used by the Metropolitan Police and was handled by Inspector Roy Hunter.

The import of the Mallion lines could be considered the most beneficial thing that had happened so far in the breed. It is interesting to note that the only two other Working Trials champions in the history of the breed were the son and the grandson of Bruin, the former being Lenlee Gladiator, who qualified CDex, UDex, TDex and PDex; the latter being Jacinto's Bolero, who qualified CDex, UDex, TDex and WDex. There is no doubt that if CCs had been on offer at the time, Bruin would probably have taken them all. He was a dog before his time.

There was a flurry of imports to follow in the years to come. All the work which had so far been done received very little recognition, because CCs were not on offer to the breed in this country. It is worth pointing out that more work had been done by the pathfinders than many people realize. So it is appropriate that the first champion to be whelped in this country was Ch. Eric of Mallion, which forms a connection between those early pathfinders and the dogs we know better by virtue of their being crowned as champions. Eric was in fact a repeat mating between Rudi Eulenspiegel of Mallion and Quinta Eulenspiegel of Mallion, the seventh repeat mating of this pair.

All the previous imports had been from Germany, but one of the most influential imports of the early 1960s was made by the Elsdens, who looked to Holland for their import. The dog they imported was Ch. Chesara Luther, a large impressive dog with plenty of bone and

W.T. Ch. Bruin of Mallion with daughters Lenlee Fern, Lenlee Delight and Lenlee Neeraum Brigitte.

17

Quinta Eulenspiegel of Mallion, owned by Mrs Chadwick.

Ch. Chesara Akilles, owned by J. Elsden.

18

substance, but perhaps, larger ears than we would like on our Rottweilers today. However, it was to be the Elsden's second import which was to have the most effect on the breed. Chesara Akilles who was bred in Sweden by R. Hamberg. This dog was to be the foundation of the modern type of Rottweiler in the UK. He was medium sized and dry, with excellent head, legs and general conformation and character. He was to sire ten UK champions, a record only equalled by the Elsden's other great stud dog, Ch. Chesara Dark Charles.

The next import of note was from Germany and this dog's name was Ch. Gamegards Bulli v d Waldachquelle. Imported by Joan Blackmore (née Woodgate) this dog excelled in head, which was clearly recognizable through his family line. He was sired by the very famous Int. Ch Bulli v Hungerbuhl, SchH.II. His influence in the breed was like a fresh wind blowing through the genetic pool. Although he died comparatively young, around five years old, he had sired some excellent dogs who were used extensively at stud. The best known of these was Jane Bloom's Ch. Janbicca The Superman, who won fourteen Challenge Certificates (a record at the time) and twice won Best of Breed at Crufts. Superman was also to prove very influential at stud. Bulli's other great son was Peter Gedge's Ch. Prince Gelert of Bhaluk, who won twelve

Ch. Gamegards Bulli v d Waldachquelle, owned by Mr and Mrs Woodgate.

19

Challenge Certificates. Gelert was an extremely handsome dog, but his influence at stud was less marked than Superman.

During the 1960s, around fifteen imports were made. Not all these were imported to contribute to the breeding programme. One dog who was specifically brought in as a potential show dog and latterly stud dog was Ch. Castor of Intisari. He was a royally bred dog, born in Denmark and imported by Mr and Mrs Radley. He was sired by Int. Ch. Farro v h Brabantpark, Sch.II and his dam was Danish Ch. Ursula PH AK. Again, he was another medium-sized dog, well constructed, very much in the same mould as Bulli. He had an excellent temperament and lived as a family pet. The main difference between him and Bulli was in head: Bulli's head was cleaner with a more defined stop. Of the two, Bulli's lines produced more winners and are more enduring. Castor twice sired two champions in a litter, his most famous son being Ch. Jagen Mr Blue. Mr Blue, though a magnificent dog himself, never really proved himself as a stud, whereas Superman, one of six champions sired by Bulli, became a prolific sire. Bulli was also the sire of Jentris Nicola Belle, who was behind so many of the best of the Poirot Kennel.

The Bulli Line

Ch. Gamegards Bulli v Waldachquelle
(BS. and KS Int. Ch. Bulli v Hungerbuhl ex Anka v Reichenbachle)
|
Ch. Prince Gelert of Bhaluk
Ch. Schutz from Gamegards
Ch. Attila Briseis
Ch. Whitebeck Touch Wood
Ch. Janbicca The Superman
Ch. Princess Malka of Bhaluk CDex UDex
|
Ch. Casses Lass of Potterspride
Ch. Poirot Camilla
Ch. Panevors Proud Kamille
Ch. Panevors Proud Kinsman
Ch. Fryerns Advocator
Ch. Ablaze of Janbicca
Ch. Isaela the Saxon
Ch. Poirot Edwina
Ch. Herburger Countess Natasha
Ch. Nobane Bianka
Ch. Jagen Blue Aria
|
Ch. Jagen Blue Moonduster
Ch. Linguard Norge
Ch. Panevors Proud Marksman of Jarot

Ch. Karla of Heranmine
Ch. Panevors Proud Chickasaw
Ch. Upend Gay Quilla
Ch. Poirot Pickwick
Ch. Poirot Led Zeppelin
Ch. Cuidado The Ladies Man
Ch. Jagen Blue Bhutia
Ch. Jagen Blue Dale
Ch. Lara Vorfelder Beauty at Lloydale
Ch. Cuidado Je T' Aime
Ch. Cuidado My Girl
Ch. Jagen Blue Chicago Bear
Ch. Rottsann Regal Romance
|
Ch. Rottsann Classic Crusader of Vormund
Ch. Rottsann Classic Gold
Ch. Herburger Touch of Brilliance from Vanhirsch
Ch. Poirot Quizzical
Ch. Rottsann Classic Centurian
Ch. Rockanoar Royal Adventure
Ch. Blue The Boy Wonder
Ch. Breckley High-Fidelity at Erland
Ch. Cuidado Annie Get Your Gun

The next import to make a major impact on the British breeding scene was Ch. Ausscot Hasso v Marchenwald, who was bred in Germany by Herr Gallas and imported by Gordon McNeill. He was very much a German type of dog, with a very impressive head, a dog who excelled on the move. He was very much loved by his owner Gordon (who was tragically to die quite young) but Hasso's blood was to produce some very good animals, not only in the UK but also in Australia, America and Canada. Hasso was sired by Int. Ch. Elko v Kastanienbaum, SchH.I.

Hasso had mixed fortunes in the ring: the judges either liked him or totally ignored him. However, he did win four CCs and six Reserve CCs and was to gain a Best of Breed placement at Crufts in 1980. Hasso sired two champions in one litter, Ch. Panevors Proud Kamille and her brother Ch. Panevors Kinsman. They were out of Gamegards Zenith of Panevor, who was one of Bulli's daughters. However, Hasso's most famous offspring was Ch. Gbos Gaytimes, who was born on 21 November 1976. She won fourteen CCs and eight Reserve CCs for her owner Helen Wilson. Her breeder was Gladys Ogilvy-Shepherd, who is the longest established of the Scottish breeders. Another notable daughter of Hasso was Ch. and Canadian Ch. Ausscot Cover Girl, who was actually bred by Gordon and was to repeat her father's success by taking Best of Breed at Crufts in 1981.

21

The next dog who must be mentioned is Ch. Rudi Anton Bali, who was born on 8 December 1979 and bred by Mr and Mrs Radcliffe. He was to become a breed record holder, with twenty-nine CCs to his credit, two Working Groups and a Best in Show, All Breeds Championship Show. He was top male show dog All Breeds 1982. Inspite of this phenomenal show record, I was never really inspired by this dog; in fact, I found him quite coarse and plain, being rough in coat and straight in stifle. However, Rudi was a great show dog, whose movement defied his conformation. It was, however, no surprise that this dog was never used to any extent by top breeders, which shows that sometimes there is very little connection between great show dogs and great producers.

This certainly did not apply to the next great dog of influence on the British show scene: Ch. Pendley Goldfinch, who was born on 27 September 1980 and bred by Joanne Yates. He won ten CCs and nine Reserve CCs Working Group and was Best of Breed at Crufts in 1984. Although he was only to win a third of the tickets that Rudi had won, this dog was used extensively by successful breeders, which is the true test of a great dog. As the saying goes, 'handsome is as handsome does'.

Ch. Pendley Goldfinch,
owned by Mr and Mrs Killick.

The same can be said of the next dog of great influence: Ch. Caprido Minstrel of Potters Pride, born 29 June 1981 and bred by Mrs Dorothy Skinner. He won a junior warrant and was top dog in 1983. Handled by his owner Mrs Slade, he won nine CCs and one Reserve CC. This tally could possibly have been a lot more had it not been for his unreliable behaviour in the show ring. He was to prove, however, a very successful stud, not only in the beauty conformation aspect, but also a phenomenal record in the absence of his dysplasia in his offspring.

One of his offspring, Jagen Dreaming Blue, was a key member of the Southern Obedience Team, a great achievement in itself, but when the team went on to win the team event at Crufts Dog Show, it was patently clear that the show dogs of today, given a chance, can still perform in the obedience arena at the highest level. Dreaming Blue was owned and trained by Gloria Hill.

Champions Bred by UK Kennels

Kennel Name	No. of Champions	Breeder
Chesara	13	Elsden
Jagen	9	Price
Rottsann	7	Brady
Borgvaale	5	Lanz
Poirot	5	Wallett
Upend	5	Butler
Cuidado	5	Pinches
Panevors	4	Hammond
Varenka	4	Rattray
Herburger	3	Hughes
Adoram	2	Quinney
Ausscot	2	McNeill
Caprido	2	Skinner
Gbos	2	Ogilvy Shepherd
Linguard	2	Simpson
Panelma	2	Bryant
Yorlanders	2	Hindley
Black Forest	2	McPhail
Vanhirsch	2	Heath

The Rottweiler in the United States of America

The first Rottweiler litter to be whelped in the USA was in 1930 by a German emigrant, Otto Denny, who was already an established breeder in his homeland. The litter was registered with a German breed club, which often happened, even after recognition by the American Kennel Club (AKC). The first Rottweiler to be registered was Stina v Felsenmeer.

23

She was later mated to Arras v Gerbermuhle, to produce the first litter to be recognized by the AKC. Thus began the great love affair between the Rottweiler and the American people. The puppies were registered under the Wellwood prefix by their breeder, August Knecht, who named them Ada, Alda, Alma and Asta. The remaining two pups were not registered with the AKC, as they were not thought to be of high enough merit.

Two other breeders bred in the 1930s. These litters were also registered with the German Rottweiler Club (ADRK). How this was achieved is a mystery. The strict breeding regulations which cover entry into the ADRK could not have been adhered to, because there was no way of checking the quality of the litter unless someone was appointed Bred Warden in the US, which is unlikely. It is probable that acceptance was based on trust. The AKC gave recognition in 1931, even without the help of a Breed Standard. The 1930s were hard times, so I think they will be forgiven for this slight oversight.

Little progress was made for thirty years. The breed was merely ticking over, a curiosity in the hands of a dedicated few. Up until the beginning of the 1950s, only about a hundred Rottweilers were registered with the AKC. After the Second World War, Rottweilers in the USA, as in Europe, started to make their mark in the obedience arena. It seems that in any country, the Rottweiler is always recognized as a working dog first and a show dog as an after thought and then as only a show dog. It is hoped that the pendulum will swing to balance equally between the two.

The first show champion in the USA was Zero, owned by Paul Jones in Idaho. His litter sister Zola, owned by Mrs Pinkerton, was to be the first bitch show champion. Mr Jones was to lead the Rottweiler to the attention of the people. A great stalwart of the breed, he was a founder member of the first breed club in the USA and handled the first Rottweiler to win the working group, possibly the best way for a new breed to gain attention. The first Rottweiler to win a best exhibit at an All Breeds Championship Show was Ch. Kato v Donnaj, bred by Laura Coonly and owned by Jan Marshall. This dog also had working qualifications CDex TD.

The USA has imported some really excellent dogs, so many in fact that it is hard to see why the constant influx of new blood is required. The dog most people think of is the great Ch. Dux v Hungerbuhl, SchHI. Although I was not fortunate enough ever to see him in the flesh, I suggest that his picture should be tattooed on the brain of every aspiring judge. He was critiqued without fault by Heinz Eberz. Work-

Am. Ch. Dux v Hungerbühl. SchH I Rom. Owned by Rodsdens Rottweilers.

ing only from photographs, I can only concur. Great dogs do not always make great studs, but Dux sired thirty-six champions, a record for the breed to date in the USA.

Before Dux, was Int. Ch. Bundessieger Harras v Sofienbusch, another fantastic dog of the best possible type with a strong will and hard temperament. He was used on only a few favoured bitches, but his influence is still undeniable, his potency incredible. Ten matings in the USA produced forty-six puppies of which seventeen were to become champions. It is unbelievable that Germany could let a dog of this quality go. Sons of Harras were also imported to the USA and they also proved of great importance. Best known was International Champion and Bundessieger and Worldsieger, Erno v Wellesweiler, an American champion. Again, it is unbelievable to an ordinary Rottweiler fanatic like me that a dog of this quality could be bought. If he were mine, I would rather sell my soul.

Then, from Holland came Ch. Oscar v H. Brabantbark, who was to have an excellent show career in the USA. Imported by Clara Hurley and Michael Grossman, when he was five years old and already a Dutch and Belgian champion, he gained his title taking a Best in Show along the way. Purchase of such outstanding dogs must be appreciated by the American Rottweiler enthusiast of today. To find such dogs is an achievement, to actually purchase these legends of the breed takes experience and sometimes disappointment, not to mention a lot of money.

From this excellent bedrock, America has bred some extremely good Rottweilers. I personally find it strange that there is still a stampede to buy any dog that has won anything in Germany. Perhaps in trying to emulate the great imports of the past, slightly less than great dogs are finding their way into the USA gene pool. Herr Alpeter, addressing a meeting in England, was asked what happened to dogs who did not fulfil the required standard for breeding in Germany (a dog can win in the show ring and still be useless for breeding). Herr Alpeter said that such dogs were sold to foreign countries - a sobering thought.

Great care must be exercised when buying in Germany as high prices gained in the sale of dogs are told and retold throughout the training clubs of Germany and as you can imagine, many German breeders want to get in on the act! The saddest story I have heard is one of a blind German boy who had a Rottweiler as his special pet. A friend of the family saw the dog and persuaded the family to enter the dog in the next show. The dog duly won his class, the boy was overjoyed and went home very happy. The next day, buyers appeared on their doorstep. It was explained that the dog was the boy's pet. Not deterred the offer price was raised and raised again, until the family could no longer turn down this fabulous offer. The buyers went away with the dog, unaware of the aftermath of unhappiness left behind. The boy was broken-hearted and inconsolable. Buying should be done with dignity by people who care for the breed. One must be sure the dog would contribute something to the USA gene pool for the improvement and betterment of the breed. Buying just for financial gain should be despised.

All dog shows where championship points are awarded are held under the rules and regulations of the American Kennel Club, who are responsible for providing qualified judges, keeping records of points and a register of pure-bred dogs. If a Rottweiler is eligible for registra-tion with the AKC, he can compete at any licensed dog show, as long as he is at least six months old and does not have a disqualifying fault. Spayed dogs are not shown. All dogs should be properly trained before they enter the show ring; they should have attended handling classes and be well used to crowds and being handled on a lead. Shows are either benched or unbenched. At benched shows, dogs should remain

Am. Ch. Rohirrim The Time Lord.

on their bench for most of the day, where the public are able to view them. At unbenched shows, you may take your dog home when you have finished in the ring. It is best to get some ring practice at the smaller classes and match meetings and iron out all problems ready for the big day when you go to a Championship Show.

What the Judge is Looking for

The judge's blueprint is the Breed Standard. The Breed Standard describes what is considered to be a perfect specimen of the breed. Also listed are definite faults, which we would hope to discourage and which are penalized heavily. The judge will go over the dog using his hands and eyes to look for any faults in conformation, but most of all to ascertain the virtues of the animal. He will then wish to see the dog in motion. This gives a clear insight into many of the structural faults and also ascertains whether the dog is sound or lame. American handlers are always smart and well turned out and show their dogs to their best advantage. The basis of showmanship is to portray a dog with physical beauty and structural soundness. A dog with intelligence and ring presence is a bonus.

Show Classes:

Dogs competing for championship points are entered in one or more of the regular classes for their breed. Schedule Classes are:

Puppy For dogs under one year old. This class may be divided into 6-9 months and 9-12 months.

Novice For dogs not having won three firsts in Novice, or in other classes (except Puppy) or any championship points.

Bred by Exhibitor For dogs who are not champions, and are owned wholly or partly by the breeder and shown by him or his family.

American Bred For all dogs (except champions) born in the USA, resulting from a mating which took place in the USA.

Open For any dog.

Winners Classes are:

Winners Dog Male winner of each class who has not been beaten in any other class, competes for Winners Dog. He receives a purple ribbon and points proportionate to the number of males present.

Reserve Winners Dog The dog who came second in the Winners Dog's original class competes with the dogs remaining in the ring, (unless he has already been defeated by one of them), for Reserve Winners. The Reserve Winner receives a purple and white ribbon and moves up to the Winners if the Winners Dog is for any reason disqualified.

Winners Bitch Exactly the same procedure is followed as for Winners Dog.

Reserve Winners Bitch Exactly the same procedure is followed as for Reserve Winners Dog.

Best of Breed The Winners Dog and the Winners Bitch compete with any champions entered for Best of Breed and winners of non-regular classes such as Veteran.

Best of Winners If the Winners Dog or Winners Bitch is awarded Best of Breed, it then becomes Best of Winners. The Winners Dog and the Winners Bitch are judged together for Best of Winners. In addition to the blue and white ribbon, the Best Winner may receive additional points if the opposite sex had an entry qualifying for higher points.

Best of Opposite Sex Following the selection of Best of Breed and Best of Winners, all the winners of the opposite sex to Best of Breed remain in the ring. From this group, Best of Opposite Sex is chosen. A red and white ribbon is awarded to the Best of Opposite Sex.

In the classes, four ribbons are usually awarded. Blue for first, red for second, yellow for third and white for fourth. Champions are not allowed to compete in the Open Classes as they do not need the points on offer. To attain champion status, the dog or bitch must win a total of fifteen points under at least three different judges. Also he must win a minimum of three points in each of two shows under different judges.

The American Rottweiler Club – Top Winners

1973 Top Three Dogs
1. Ch. Rodsden's Duke du Trier
2. Ch. Rowdy's Rinky Dink
3. Ch. Rodsden's Kato v Donnaj CDX

1973 Top Three Bitches
1. Ch. Bimpse v d Gaarn
2. Ch. Srigo's Madchen v Kurtz
3. Ch. Baerbel v Odenwald

1974 Top Three Dogs
1. Ch. Uwe v Kursaal
2. Ch. Titan Sujon
3. Ch. Rodsden's Rough Diamond

1974 Top Three Bitches
1. Ch. Srigo's Watch My Smoke
2. Ch. Rodsden's Rally
3. Asta v Fortswald

1975 Top Three Dogs
1. Ch. Burley v Morgen Carroll CD
2. Ch. Duke's Derek v Altmeister
3. Ch. Erno v Ingenhof

1975 Top Three Bitches
1. Ch. Riegele's Agreta Maid
2. Ch. Brady Haserway v Haus Kalbas
3. Ch. Bea Mathilda v Haus Kalbas

1976 Top Three Dogs
1. Ch. Burley v Morgen Carroll CD
2. Ch. Radio Ranch Axel v Notara
3. Ch. Centurion's Che v d Barr

1976 Top Three Bitches
1. Ch. Panamint Pakt v Rheintal
2. Ch. Christa v Odenwald
3. Ch. Riegele's Agreta Maid

1977 Top Three Dogs
1. Ch. Centurion's Che v d Barr
2. Ch. Burley v Morgen Carroll CD
3. Ch. Phaedra's Amax of Sunnyside

1977 Top Three Bitches
1. A/B Ch. Andan Indy Pendence v Paulus
2. Ch. Panamint Pakt v Rheintal
3. Ch. Vala v Kursaal

1978 Top Three Dogs
1. Ch. Phaedra's Amax of Sunnyside
2. Ch. Gatstuberget's Eskil Jarl CD
3. Ch. Panamint Otso v Kraewel UD

1978 Top Three Bitches
1. Ch. Haserway's Razzle Dazzle
2. Ch. Chelsea de Michaela
3. Ch. V Gailingen's Welkerhaus Cia

1979 Top Three Dogs
1. Ch. Oscar v h Brabantpark
2. Ch. Rodsden's Ansel v Brabant
3. Ch. Rodsden's Bruin v Hungerbuhl CD

1979 Top Three Bitches
1. A/B Ch. Andan Indy Pendence v Paulus
2. Ch. Radio Ranch's Christmas Spirit
3. Ch. De Riemer's Sjefke CD

1980 Top Three Dogs
1. Ch. Erno v d Gaarn
2. Ch. Bethel Farm's Apollo
3. Ch. Quanto v h Brabantpark

1980 Top Three Bitches
1. Ch. Erdelaid Astraea CD
2. Ch. Karly v Medeah CD
3. Ch. Reza Birs v Hause Schumann

1981 Top Three Dogs
1. Ch. Rodsden's Ansel v Brabant
2. Ch. Donnaj Green Mountain Boy
3. Ch. Rodsden's Bruin v Hungerbuhl CDX

1981 Top Three Bitches
1. Ch. Trollegen's Kyra v Sonnenhaus
2. Ch. Radio Ranch's Christmas Spirit
3. Ch. Erdelied Astraea CD

1982 Top Three Dogs
1. Ch. Donnaj Green Mountain Boy
2. Ch. Rhomark's Axel v Lerchenfeld
3. Ch. Maximillian Schwartzgruen

1982 Top Three Bitches
1. Ch. RC's Magnum Force v Ursa
2. Ch. Beaverbrook Brenna v Fable
3. Ch. Trollegen's Kyra v Sonnenhaus

Best in Show Winners – AKC All Breed Shows

1971	AM/CAN Ch. Rodsden's Kato v Donnaj CDex TD (5/29/71)
	Ch. Rodsden's Duke du Trier (5/30/72) (2 BIS)
1975	Ch. Erno v Ingenhof
	Ch. Rodsden's Duke du Trier (2 BIS)
	Ch. Duke's Derek v Altmeister
1976	Ch. Shearwater Cochise
1979	Ch. Donnaj vt Yankee of Paulus CDex
	Ch. Oscar v h Brabantpark
	Ch. Rodsden's Bruin v Hungerbuhl (3 BIS)
1980	Ch. Rodsden's Bruin v Hungerbuhl (3 BIS)
	Ch. Van Tieleman's Cisco
1981	Ch. Rodsden's Bruin v Hungerbuhl (2 BIS)
1982	Ch. Rhomark's Axel v Lerchenfeld

The Rottweiler in Scandinavia

Norway

The first Rottweiler in Norway arrived in the year 1910, but it was not until 1919 that a bitch called Florrie, who had been originally imported from Sweden, was registered. Her importer, E. Palmguist, then became a founder member of the Norwegian Rottweiler Club which was founded in 1933. It is interesting to note that the Norwegian Rottweiler Club also founded the Norwegian Kennel Club.

It is unusual for Norwegian Rottweiler owners to have large kennels. Rottweilers usually live as family pets or working dogs. Norwegians are keen to train their dogs and Rottweilers are used for many purposes, from mountain rescue to drug detection. Their working ability in Norway is rated very highly. I have always found the Rottweilers in Norway to be of very stable disposition, and this is probably because the Rottweilers live as family pets, with a stable home life.

Norway, Sweden and Finland were, until recently, rabies free and show dogs from Scandinavia were entered in all three countries. Unfortunately, rabies has now been detected in Finland.

Nor. Ch. Jagen Blue Star of Zarstø, owned by Mr and Mrs Andersen.

The Nordic Championship Show for Rottweilers is rotated between the three different countries. On the first day of the show, working trial tests are held, reflecting the interest in this aspect of the breed. On the second day, the Breed Show itself is held. This show is the highlight of the year for Rottweiler enthusiasts and it was my privilege to be able to handle a UK import to win Best of Breed here in 1986. On entering the ring, all dogs are checked and absentees noted. The dogs stand in numerical order and the judge then looks at every exhibit and examines teeth and, in the case of dogs, testicles. During his examination he makes notes on a pad. The class is then excused and the entries return to the ring one at a time in numerical order to be judged individually. The judge goes over the dog and then assesses him on the move, at the end of which the dog receives a written critique and a grading, which is symbolized by different coloured ribbons: red for first, blue for second and yellow for third. Only the firsts are allowed to return to compete for class placements. In other words, if you do not receive a first grading, that is as far as you go although you get a written critique, so that you at least know why you didn't make the placings.

The winner of the open classes usually receives a certificate, which is the equivalent to the Challenge Certificate in the UK. Reserve Certificates are also available and more than one may be awarded. Then there is a champion class and the winner of the champion class meets the winner of the Certificate and Reserve Certificate to compete for Best of Sex. Then the dog and the bitch compete for Best of Breed.

Incidentally, a first grading would be awarded to a typical dog of good conformation, with only minor faults, a very good representative of the breed. A second grading is a good representative of the breed with no serious faults. A dog that gains a third prize is a dog that lacks quality and is not perfect in construction, but one that still cannot be called a poor specimen.

I have found Norwegian shows to be very relaxed and Norwegian people accept the decisions of the judge very well, which is to their credit, for with the grading system and every dog receiving a critique, everyone feels they have achieved something.

Norway has always looked to Sweden for breeding influence. The first great influence from Sweden was the Fandangos Kennel. It was, however, Norwegian Ch. Ponto who sired the famous Int. Ch. Fandangos Fairboy. Ponto not only influenced Norwegian and Swedish Rottweiler history, but also the UK's through his grandson Ch. Chesara Akilles, who was to sire ten UK champions.

The Swedish influence has continued up to the present day, where

Int. and Nor. Ch. Zarstø's Bunny.

the Faunus Kennel has a great influence on the breeding stock in Norway. One such kennel is the Zarstøs Kennel, owned by Mr and Mrs L. and E. Anderson, who have produced some top winners in the last few years, the most famous of which is Int. and Norwegian Ch. Korad Bellinas Zari, who was the top winning Rottweiler in Norway in 1984 and 1985. Her daughter, International and Nordic Winner 1987, Ch. Zarstø's Bunny, who was top winning Rottweiler in 1988-89. She was sired by Swedish import Norwegian Ch. Korad Bersgardens Ramus. Of the males in Norway, one of the best of recent years that I have particularly liked was Norwegian Ch. Chubby of Rottmann, although the latest star on the show scene seems to be international and Norwegian winner Mellomossens Marco Polo.

Other kennels of note in Norway are the Kimuras Kennels, owned by Mr and Mrs Lindstrome, the Dixi Gaarden Kennels and the Valheins Kennels. All are making significant contributions to the breed at this time.

One of the latest imports into Norway is a German-bred dog called Kolja v Bakkes. This dog was originally imported into the UK by me. He is a V1 winner, the highest rated German dog ever to be imported

Int. and Nor. Ch. Mellomossens Marco Polo.

Kolja v Bakkes, owned by Mr and Mrs Andersen.

into the UK. Having sired one litter in the UK, he was then sent on to Norway. Since being in Norway, he has been used to stud not only by the Norwegians but also by the top Swedish kennel Faunus, which is owned and run by Gun Berquist. It is too early to estimate the value of this dog at stud in Scandinavia, but the litter sired in the UK has produced winners at Championship Show level, not only in the UK but also in Australia and Norway itself, for one of his sons Jagen Blue Brutally Handsome, was exported to Norway to the kennel of Mr T Lindstrome prior to Kolja's arrival in Norway. This dog has already won a CC and in-show awards. His dam was the well-known Eika v Barrenstein BH AD EJS (1986). One of Kolja's daughters, Zarsto's Fit For Fight has already won nine CCs at 16 months old.

Norwegian Rottweilers are soundly built, of good size and stable temperament, which probably explains why they are in such great demand not only as family companions but working dogs. Many Norwegians participate in mountain rescue, which is usually carried out in deep snow. Rottweilers seem to excel at this work. It is a large country with a small population and so it is very easy to get lost. Even on the main routes over the mountains, we have travelled many miles

Nor. Ch. Valheim's Ikaros.

36

through snow blizzards without seeing a single house on the horizon. This is why Norwegians take this training so seriously. Indeed, special clubs have been set up which concentrate entirely on mountain rescue.

It is this special blend of solid conformation, mental ability and participation by owners who exploit the best from their dogs that will keep the Rottweiler one of the most favoured dogs in Norway.

Sweden

The Swedish Rottweiler Club (AFR) was founded in 1968. Today, it has a membership of over one thousand. As with Norway, breeding restrictions are very tight. Hips and elbows must have been X-rayed and have received excellent results, but further more, all dogs must participate in the Swedish mental test. As in Germany, all results from these tests are published.

The first Rottweiler to be registered in Sweden was a bitch Syda v Karlstor, registered in 1914. However, the first dog to be imported to have any major influence was Arbo Torfwerk. He was imported into Sweden in 1921 and was litter brother to winner Arco Torfwerk. This

Faunus Cinderella.

The author with his Best of Breed and Best Opposite Sex at the 1990 Stockholm International Show. Left: B.O.B. Int and Nor Ch. Faunus Bullit. Right: B.O.S. Zarstøs Fit for Fight.

blood-line was particularly helpful to the early breeders because the line was in-bred, his parents being brother and sister of excellent breeding and so consequently true to type. Arbo's most famous son was dual Champion Aspnas Bjorn Skks. Bjorn shone brightly in everything he was asked to do, not only at shows but also at trials. He was a very accomplished tracking dog and gained recognition from the Swedish police for his achievements.

The breed in Sweden was off to a tremendous start and from this position of strength, Swedish people have produced over the years some very good Rottweilers. Imports were almost exclusively from Germany, but it is obvious that much thought had been put into their acquisitions, for the next dog to be imported was Ossman v Frankofurtia in 1930. This dog's line went directly back to Arbo's more famous brother Arco Torfwerk. Ossman was not shown but became a stud dog, – most useful as breeders in Sweden would continue line-breeding.

During the 1960s, Sweden's top stud dog was Ch. Fandangos Fairboy. Along with International, Nordic and Finnish Ch. Fandangos Faruk, they have cast their influence right across Europe, America and Australia. The most successful show dog of all time in the whole of

Scandinavia was Ch. Bergsgardens King of Sweden who was owned by Rolf Soderlund.

Probably one of the best-known characters in Swedish Rottweiler history is Mrs Gerd Hyden, who is an international judge and breeds Rottweilers under the Saltsjoborg prefix. Her kennel has won the Hamilton Award for the Swedish Kennel who produces top quality breeding. This award has also been won by the Fandangos Kennel and Bergsgardens Kennel.

Other kennels of note in Swedish history are: Nordangens, Fandangos, Bergsgardens, Lyngsjons, Odels, Aviemores and Faunus. The Faunus Kennel has dominated the Swedish scene over the last few years, one of their top winners being Faunus Bullit. The breed in Sweden is strong and can compete with any country. It has been built on a solid bedrock of good dogs and breeding control, with a strong emphasis on mentality.

Finland

The first police dogs to come to Finland were in 1908. They were German Shepherds, Dobermanns and probably Rottweilers.

The first Rottweiler to be registered by the Kennel Club of Finland was a male and his name was Hammarbys Puck (KC Reg. No. 6206). He was bred in Stockholm and was owned by Capt. Gustafaspegren in Helsinki. Puck was born on 3 January 1923. The first prefix to be registered was Kiikkuniemi in 1933.

Many Rottweilers were imported prior to the Second World War but their influence on the breed today is negligible because, as in other countries, the war so seriously destroyed the breeding programme. During the war, many working dogs helped with the defence effort. The majority were German Shepherds but it is known that Rottweilers did contribute.

The first Rottweilers in Finland to gain their championship titles were H P Hn Belzebub and H P Hn Barry, both in 1948. H P Hn Tomi was the third Rottweiler to achieve the title in Finland and was also the first bitch to do so, again in 1948. Belzebub was owned by Mr Olavi Pasanen and his wife Maria, who in later years bred many well-known dogs under the Heidenmoor prefix.

This completes the three Nordic countries, where it is possible to make up an international champion. To gain the title of Nordic Champion, it is necessary to be a champion in the country of origin and also to achieve at least one certificate in each of the other countries. To gain the International Champion title, it is necessary to win the championship in the country of origin and an international ticket in two of the other participating countries, one in your own country. There must be one year and one day between the first and last, under two different judges, which is no mean achievement. However, before the International Champion title is awarded, it is necessary for the Rottweiler to pass an obedience and tracking test. Therefore, one can say that a Rottweiler who achieves international championship status in the Nordic countries has to be a Rottweiler of the very highest standard.

The Rottweiler in Holland

The first record of a Rottweiler being exhibited in Holland was in 1910. This is not surprising as Holland and Germany are close neighbours. In view of this, one would expect the breed to have firmly established itself long ago. However, the outbreak of war caused an anti-Germanic feeling across Europe, especially in Holland, where this feeling prevented the further growth of this German breed.

The Dutch people love working dogs. Although their favourite dog is possibly the Bouvier des Flandres, real interest began to grow in the Rottweiler in the 1960s. Improvements of the breed have been no problem, for the Dutch have access to the best stud lines available in a German gene pool. Some outstanding dogs have been produced in Holland, the Brabantpark and the Triomfator Kennels being the most famous.

The most outstanding dog to be produced in Holland is surely Mr G. Kuijpers Int. Ch. Duuck v d Nedermolen. Duuck has been Club Champion in the Netherlands in 1982, 1983 and 1984. In addition to this, he has crossed the border gaining not only a ZPT qualification, (*see* Appendix 1), but also SchH III. In 1981, he won the title World Champion. A truly magnificent dog both physically and mentally.

Dutch kennels often travel to Germany for the larger shows. In 1987, Bulli Triomfator won the open class at the Bundessieger, gaining VI (*see* Appendix 1), while Dunja Triomfator won the open bitch class, both these animals are owned and bred by Miss Gruter, whose kennel is situated in Zunderdorp. Both animals were the only Rottweilers in the open class to gain a V rating. The bitch sieger class was also won by Miss Gruter with Hera v d Kathaarens Winstler, who is an NL and Lux Champion. As can be seen, the Dutch do more than hold their own in the strong German classes, even at this level.

All dogs who are bred in Holland have to be X-rayed for hip

Ned. and Int. Ch. Duuck v d Nedermolen, Weltsieger 1981, SchH II III. Owned by G. Kuijpers.

dysplasia and must have a normal or near normal rating. They must also pass a character test which is organized by the Netherlands Rottweiler Club. Incidentally, bitches may not be bred from more than once a year and strictly not when under the age of two years old and dogs of two years and under may not be used at stud. It is also necessary for all breeding stock to have been graded at least 'very good' by two different judges at official shows. It would be nice to see this regulation enforced in all countries by the individual Rottweiler Clubs. The Dutch, second to the Germans, probably have the strictest breeding regime in Europe.

The Breed Club takes an active role in all things, including inspection of litters to help with the resale of puppies from litters which are bred within the Club's jurisdiction.

The Rottweiler in Ireland

Ireland as a country is run by two governments. Since Northern Ireland is part of the UK, all things pertaining to dogs come under the UK

Kennel Club's jurisdiction, while in the south, or Eire, dogs must be entered with the Irish Kennel Club.

Northern Ireland has two shows where CCs are on offer to Rottweilers, the Northern Ireland Rottweiler Club's Championship Show and the Belfast All Breeds Championship Show. Exhibitors in the south however have twenty All Breed Championship Shows and one Club Show where green stars are on offer. Green stars are allocated at these shows and are made up on a points basis. Each breed has an index figure, which is equivalent to the number of dogs required to be actually exhibited (not just entered), to gain a five point green star. For entries over 20 per cent above the index figure actually shown, another point will be added, up to a maximum of ten points. Forty points are required for a champion and four of these green stars must be majors, which means they must have five points or more.

Apart from the Club shows north and south, the highlights of the year must be the Belfast Championship Show in the north and the St Patrick's Day Show in the south. The St Patrick's Day Show is always

Ch. and Irish Ch. Jagen Blue Moonduster, owned by Watt and McCurley.

held in Dublin and all green stars awarded are usually guaranteed majors, which usually encourages a large entry.

In the south, August is the busiest month of the entire year for the Irish show goers. Six Championship Shows are held in three weeks. The third week in August usually sees the start of what is known as the Munster Circuit, four Championship Shows in seven days. Irish show goers look forward to the Munster Circuit. There is a certain sense of camaraderie where people travel from show to show; aside from the serious work of showing dogs, it is also a great social event with many new friendships being forged in these few weeks. The fact that it is possible to make up an Irish champion in one week draws not only a high proportion of exhibitors from the north, but also many exhibitors from the UK who travel by ferry and aeroplane to take part in what is known as The Circuit. Only one Irish-owned dog has won a UK title, Ch. Jagen Blue Chicago Bear, and only one Irish-owned bitch has won her UK title, Ch. and Irish Ch. Jagen Blue Moonduster. One dog who was already a UK champion was exported to Ireland: Ch. and Irish Ch. Cuidado the Dandy.

Ch. Jagen Blue Chicago Bear, owned by Mr and Mrs McCullum.
Ten times BIS All Breeds.

Irish Champions

Name of Dog	Date Cert. Issued	Owner
Nedraw Ailsa (GB)	11. 2. 81	Mr F. Warden
Borgvaale Christian (GB)	1.11. 82	Mr F. Warden
Nedraw Athos (GB)	12.11. 82	Mrs G. Gibbons
The Happy Hooker Of Nemorez (GB)	6. 7. 84	Mrs R. Taylor
Manzai Igor (GB)	10. 9. 84	M/s Loughlin and Harris
Nedraw Corona (GB)	5. 11. 84	Mr and Mrs M. Murphy
Royal Renagade (GB)	5. 11. 84	Mr and Mrs E. McKeown
Mialgo National Velvet Atannoca	18.7. 85	Mrs A. Carroll
Mialgo Roar of Thor	18. 7. 85	Mr Cooke and Miss Mullins
Clear Commandment Of Janbicca (GB)	10. 9. 85	Mr J. Bond
Cottonwood Super Trouper (GB)	25. 9. 85	Mr J. Lettherd
Nedraw Freebotter (GB)	5. 11. 85	Mr and Mrs M Murphy
Janbicca Perseus (GB)	17. 12. 85	Mr J. Bond
Nedraw Waltons Wonder (GB)	9. 5. 86	Mr F. Warden
Cuidado The Dandy (GB)	5. 9. 86	Mr and Mrs B. White
Taroh Oriel (GB)	11. 2. 87	Mr T. Kelly
Vanhirsch Black Velvet	11. 2. 87	Mr J. Payne
Jagen Blue Raindancer (GB)	5. 5. 88	Mr Watt and Mr McCurley
Manzai Tracy	9. 7. 87	Mr L. Farrell
Jagen Blue Moonduster	5. 5. 88	Mr Watt and Mr McCurley
Annoca Bold 'n' Brazen	28. 9. 88	Mr L. Farrell
Thor of Thunder	2. 11.88	Mr Barri Orr
Baron Jack	21.11. 89	Mr G. O'Shea
Kes of Blackskull	21.2. 90	Mr and Mrs I. Dickson
Jagen Blue Belinda	1990	Rev G. McQuillan

The Rottweiler in Australia

In 1958, Mr and Mrs Mummery decided they would try to import some stock of the very best blood-lines into Australia. Mr Mummery at the time was a police dog trainer. He had seen his first Rottweiler in the UK whilst visiting a police dog training centre and he was greatly impressed with his working ability. He decided to import a dog named Balthasar of Mallion, whose sire was Rudi Eulenspiegel of Mallion and whose dam was Quinta Eulenspiegel of Mallion. Unfortunately, tragedy struck and the dog was to die on board ship through heat exhaustion. This was a tragic loss to Australia because the blood-lines would have been extremely useful.

In 1962, Capt. Roy-Smith arrived in Australia, bringing some dogs with him. The bitch, Rintelna the Chatelaine, was to whelp the first litter born in Australia, having been mated prior to leaving the UK. The bitch produced six puppies, but Capt. Roy-Smith destroyed all but one.

Aust. Ch. Stromhall Torrey, owned by Stromhall Kennels.

His explanation was that he could find no suitable homes for the other puppies. The Mummerys therefore placed an order for a bitch from the next litter, which was born on 13 July 1963.

In the meantime, the Mummerys planned another import. This was to be Pilgrimsway Loki. This dog was then mated to Rintelna the Fatale, who had been a puppy purchased from Capt. Roy-Smith. This litter, born on 5 December 1965, was to be the first born in Victoria and was registered under the Heatherglen prefix. Australian Rottweiler history had begun.

Mr Mummery then imported a bitch called Lenlee Gail, who was by W T Ch. Bruin of Mallion, out of Lenlee Neeruam Brigitte CDex UDex, a bitch of impeccable working lines. Gail was mated several times to Loki, the offspring proving influential in the development of the breed in Australia.

The first Rottweiler to be imported from Germany came via the UK, owing to very strict quarantine regulations. Her name was Catja v d Flugschneise. In the time she spent in the UK, Catja was mated to Ch. Castor of Intisari. This litter was whelped in the UK and several puppies remained here, while four accompanied their mother to Australia. The puppies that were to remain in the UK, although shown, achieved no obvious success, either in the show ring or as breeding prospects. However, their litter mates in Australia were apparently used extensively.

Imports into Australia today are legion, coming not only from the UK and Germany but also from Finland, Italy and the USA. I feel this is possibly not a good thing at this present time, when every spectrum of Rottweiler size, shape and type can still be found in the show ring: further expansions of the gene pool can only have a destructive effect. It is possibly that the judging system in Australia, where almost all judges are all-rounders and are passed to judge at group level, has not helped the development of type in Australia. Another very unhelpful element breedwise is the ease in which champions are made up. In Australia, championships are gained on a point system and it is feasible, however unlikely, that a Rottweiler Champion could be made up without actually meeting a member of his own breed in competition. Possibly more champions are made up in one year in Australia

Aust. Ch. Stromhall Liebschen, owned by Stromhall Kennels.

than the total achieved in the UK since the breed's first introduction. This cannot be a good thing. The word 'champion' by definition, means 'he who conquers all'; it should not mean 'he who has driven the furthest'. This mass grading of champions takes away the achievements gained by the dogs who are true champions.

Having said all that, there have been some very nice dogs bred in Australia, not only achieving high show placements, but also major obedience awards. One of the first such dogs was Mrs Hall's Stromhall Torrey CH CDex UDex TD. Torrey was also a very good sire, producing many excellent offspring.

When considering showing dogs in Australia, it must be realized that the country has a total area of three million square miles and is divided into five mainland states and two territories, plus the island state of Tasmania. At the moment, there are six Rottweiler clubs in Australia: the Rottweiler Club of Victoria, which is the oldest club; the Rottweiler Club of New South Wales; the Rottweiler Club of Queensland; the Rottweiler Club of Western Australia; the Rottweiler Club of South Australia and the Northern Territory Rottweiler Club. All these clubs are extremely active and put on many events for their members. Carting is very popular, as is agility, working trials and latterly Schutzhund trials. There are many dogs in Australia now who hold Schutzhund titles, which have been gained in Australia under German judges. General obedience is taught by most of the Rottweiler clubs to new handlers as a public service exercise and this early training sometimes inspires people to go on to do greater things.

The future of the breed in Australia looks to be in good hands, although some moves towards getting a clearer definition of type must be made. This is a very difficult task in such a large country. However, all the Rottweiler clubs do have a National Council to oversee all affairs dealing with Rottweilers. I feel the greatest contribution the National Council could make to the Rottweiler in Australia is the stabilizing of type, but in the present climate, with a flood of imports from various destinations, this will be all the more difficult.

All people intending to breed from their dogs in Australia are strongly recommended to participate in the hip dysplasia scoring scheme. At the time of X-ray, the dog's ear is tattooed and the X-ray is marked with that tattoo number so that there is always proof of the dog's soundness. It is also possible to have your dog's bite and eyes certified by the veterinary surgeon while the dog is sedated. The Victoria Rottweiler Club actually owns its own tattoo machine and members apply for a number from the secretary of the club. This system is streets ahead of the slap-happy way tests are carried out in the UK, where the whole system of hip dyplasia testing is open to abuse.

Another service rendered by the Victorian Rottweiler Club is the 'litter expected' notice. Members are able to fill in a form to notify the Club that a litter is due to be whelped. On this form, the applicant signs a declaration that, to the best of his knowledge, the sire and dam do not suffer from hip dysplasia, entropion, undershot or overshot jaw, wrymouth, incomplete dentition, extreme shyness of or viciousness towards people, total absence of tan marking, yellow bird-of-prey eyes or eyes that are not the same colour, white markings. The hip scores of both parents are then given and all this information is published in the Club magazine, not only to assist people in the purchase of quality puppies, but also for the general information and education of members.

Some of the best-known kennels in Australia are: Angepena, Anverdons, Auslese, Brabantsia, Beirnstut, Cardweil, Heatherglen, Kalatara, Kerusgal, Korobeit, Lamez, Metzkers, Morweiler, Murraval, Muzairib, Ormslee, Robstans, Rodonburg, Romawi, Rotset, Rottser, Rotvel, St Arkhund, Schaden, Stromhall, Tarawa, Tarquinian, Tayverka, Utz, Yarrawon, Zanbax. For those I've missed, I apologize.

The majority of these kennels are in the Victoria area. One of the reasons for this is that up until the early 1970s Victoria was the only state to stage classes for Rottweilers. Up until that time entries would be relatively small, possibly less that ten at most shows. As entries started to grow, several stars started to appear in the show ring. Ch. Uplands Lados had an extremely impressive track record: he won the challenge not only at the Melbourne Royal, but also at the Sydney Royal. In the early 1980s, Ch. Tarquinian Ambassador and his sister Ch. Tarquinian Adante scooped over ninety CCs between them. Other good winners are Tayvelka Noble Marcus and Ch. Schaden Cheyenne and the bitch Ch. Saarlund Quanabie Mist, who was a grandaughter of UK Ch. Gamegards Bulli v d Waldachquelle.

As I mentioned before, Ch. Stromhall Torrey CDex UD, TD, was a prolific winner winning Best in Show at the 1983 Rottweiler Club Show. Torrey had been a group winner on three occasions, one of which was the Sydney Royal. This dog would clearly have been a dual champion had he not been killed at an early age, constituting a great loss to the Australian show scene.

Australian Ch. Anderjays Our Marcus won Best Exhibit at the 1988 Rottweiler Club at the Victoria Championship Show and went on to win runner-up in show at the 1988 Melbourne Royal Show. Ch.

Aust. Ch. Muzairib Bobby McGee, owned by T. Truscott.

Schaden Illiad has won a Best in Show at Championship Show level and has also been the top winning dog on two occasions.

The show scene in Australia is very active, as are the obedience trials and latterly the fast-growing Schutzhund sport. Registrations are still growing and have not yet peaked out. The breed, however, is in good hands and can learn by mistakes made elsewhere.

The Rottweiler in New Zealand

The early history of the Rottweiler in New Zealand is somewhat hazy. What we do know is that the first Rottweiler to be registered with the New Zealand Club was Auslese Montrachet, who was imported from Australia. He was whelped on 17 March 1970, so the history of the Rottweiler in New Zealand is in its infancy, barely twenty years old.

This dog was soon followed by another Australian import, whose name was Asgardweiler Winston, whelped on 14 November 1971. This dog was to become New Zealand's first recorded Rottweiler champion. Two more Australian imports from the Auslese Kennel followed soon after: Auslese Lafite and Auslese Echezeaux.

It is thought that the first bitch to be imported was from England, Attila Bathsheba, who was imported in whelp to a good dog, Upend Gallant Alf. The bitch was apparently diverted to New Zealand because all the quarantine kennels in Australia were full. The litter born to this bitch on 24 July 1975 was the first to be whelped in New Zealand. The second bitch to gain her New Zealand title was Ch. Kinlock Sachsen, who, again, was imported from Australia. The third bitch to be imported was Kerusgal Black Czarina, born 24 February 1976. The fourth import into New Zealand, again from Australia, was probably the best of the early imports. A very good bitch, known as NZ Ch. Heatherglen Hebe. Hebe was to win the Bitch CC in the 1976, 1977 and 1978 Nationals.

The two most prominent dogs around this time were Korobeit Hero and Grossheim Igor, who had been imported by Mr Alf Church of the Standhalf Kennels. This dog was to sire NZ Ch. Great Valour of Firgorran, who was to be the sire of the first Rottweiler to take Best in Show at Tux Nationals, Ch. Salbo of Firgorran. Mr Bernie Cok imported Chesara Dark Igor in October 1976. He was by Chesara Dark Warlord out of Ch. Chesara Byxfield Akela and around that time Chesara Dark Helen was imported. She was sired by Chesara Rebel of Alastel, out of Tara Triomfator from Chesara.

The next group of imports was made by Mr C. W. Bradley, the first

50

NZ Ch. Yorlanders Migrant.

being Heatherglen Beautique, sired by Adoram Matheson out of Heatherglen Freda, and originally imported from the UK into Australia. The second import was NZ Ch. Heatherglen Faber, again imported from Australia and, again, sired by Adoram Matheson, this time out of Heatherglen Adda. The third import was Heatherglen Danni, who was sired by Chesara Dark Boris (who had been imported from the UK into Australia) out of Heatherglen Ina. The fourth import, Heatherglen Lucette, was sired by Korobeit Hud, out of Chesara Dark Wishful, who had been imported from the UK. The fifth import was Peterae Lynnes Star, and last was Lamez Caesar, both imported from Australia.

Mr and Mrs K. Newell, who live in Auckland, imported NZ Ch. Javictreva Double Dutch from the UK. She was bred by Noreen and Trevor Simmons and her sire was Chesara Dark Roisterer, her dam Javictreva Kaleidoscope. This bitch was to take Best Bitch and Best of Breed at the 1980 Nationals.

From these early imports, rapid progress has been made, although large ears and weak heads are the most common faults to be found in New Zealand stock. It is to the credit of the New Zealand breeders that

NZ Ch. Jagen Blue Matchmaker, owned by A. Franks.

these faults were recognized and several imports from the UK were made specifically to help with this problem, notably NZ Ch. Upend Gallant Zeberdee (bred by Barbara Butler), NZ Ch. Yorlanders Migrant (bred by Kath and Brian Hindley), NZ Ch. Jagen Blue Matchmaker and NZ Ch. Nivelle Elite, who all sired some excellent stock, some of which was exported to Australia and at the time of writing, has taken Best in Show at Club Championship Show level. All of these imports from the UK not only sired good stock but also gained their New Zealand Championships. Migrant did particularly well, winning several Best in Shows at All Breed Championship Shows and won the title of New Zealand's Top Utility Dog. He was sired by Jagen Blue Andante out of Ch. Chesara Dark Hunters Dawn of Yorlander.

Some of the most notable dogs bred in New Zealand include NZ Ch. Blair Gowrie Bayla Lugossi CDex UDex. Bayla was the first CDex and UDex Rottweiler in New Zealand – a great achievement. He was owned and trained by Alison Franks. Also, Ch. Great Valour of Firgorran, who was to sire Ch. Salvo of Firgorran, the first Rottweiler to take Best in Show at the Tux Nationals. Nz Ch. Sanduka Midnite Manifesto is also a Best in Show winner, as are Ch. Anton v Storhund and Ch. Teutonis of Firgorran.

Between 1974 and 1975, there were just two Rottweilers registered with the New Zealand Kennel Club. By 1983/84, there were 388. This can be explained in part by the large numbers of dogs that were imported initially, but it is clear that the breed has really taken off and is now firmly established in the top ten most popular breeds in New Zealand. In 1988, 2,019 Rottweilers were registered from 204 litters, which seems an incredible amount of Rottweilers per head of population. It is hoped that this phenomenal increase will soon level out.

The breed clubs in New Zealand are very active and are keen to encourage obedience and working trials activities. It is obvious that the breed clubs will have a very difficult time in the next decade. Fortunately for the breed, there are enough dedicated people who will be available to care for its welfare.

The Rottweiler in South Africa

The Rottweiler's appearance in South Africa is sketchy. It is known that Rottweilers had been imported prior to the Second World War, probably by German and Dutch immigrants. Again, not much is known, but it is thought they were probably pets or purely working dogs. However, during the late 1950s/early 1960s, a great deal of interest was generated and, by the 1970s the breed was firmly established with the South African Kennel Club. By 1980, registrations were around the 3,000 mark. It is clear that all around the world, Rottweilers seem to have been discovered all at the same time. By 1985, figures for Rottweiler registration had gone over 4,000. It is thought likely that more than this have been bred and not registered, simply used as guard dogs by the booming security industry in South Africa.

One of the first kennels to establish itself as a consistent winner in the show ring was the Tankerville Kennel. This kennel's top winning inmate was SA Ch. Tankerville Digby. Digby was the first Rottweiler in South Africa to win Best in Show at an All Breeds Show. He was sired by Ch. Upend Gallant Luke, who was bred by Barbara Butler in the UK. His dam was Tankerville Heidi, who was Rottweiler Bitch of the Year from 1979–1983.

Another long-established kennel in South Africa is St Tuttston, owned and run by Denise Tutt and, latterly, her daughter. In fact, SA Ch. St Tuttston Bastian of Tankerville was the foundation stud dog of

SA Ch. St Tuttston Lando,
owned by D.E. Tutt.

the Tankerville Kennels and was probably responsible for bringing the breed to the notice of the general public. During his show career, he won in excess of sixty Best of Breeds. It is good that both these kennels, who were established right at the start of the breed's development, are still active today.

The Von Sophias Kennel is probably the most successful present-day kennel. Kennel handler, Sue Hoffman, attends almost every Championship Show in South Africa. The number of miles that it is necessary to travel in order to accomplish this are simply phenomenal. It is not unusual for the Von Sophias Kennel to turn out seventeen Rottweilers at one show. The Von Sophias Kennel's greatest achievement was winning Dogmoor Dog of The Year 1988 with SA Ch. Von Sophias Wilbur. In my opinion Wilbur is not the best dog in the Von Sophias Kennel, despite his success, since he is quite plain in head. My two particular favourites would be SA Ch. Von Sophias Bulli and SA Ch. Von Sophias Jonnifer, who I personally consider to be capable of winning anywhere in the world.

The Dogmoor competition invites a dog and a bitch from each breed to compete. When Wilbur achieved this great win, the bitch who was invited was SA Ch. Vagabond v Kabou, owned by Kathy and Roger Bouton, an up-and-coming kennel from Port Elizabeth.

SA Ch. Jagen Blue Ragged Robin, owned by Mr and Mrs Lower.

In Johannesburg, the Sheidal Kennels have imported Ch. Jagen Blue Ragged Robin of Sheidal from the UK. This dog not only became a very good show dog, but also an excellent working dog and great stock getter. He was sired by Ch. Panelma The Adventurer, out of Ch. Jagen Blue Aria. Many imports ar now being made from Germany. Their influence is yet to be fully evaluated.

To make a champion in South Africa, it is necessary to win a total of five points. These have to be won under five different judges, with at least one CC being awarded outside one's home province. If an entry attracts more than ten dogs, the CC is then worth two points. Dogs who are already champions have to compete in the champions class. Personally, I do not think the number of entries that are made at South African shows justify champion classes. Compared with the number of dogs who are registered, entries to shows are quite small: fifty to a hundred entries compared with 3,000 registrations for 1986.

Another competition, held annually, is the Heads and Tails Top Dog competition, which is run by a magazine. Once again, this was won by SA Ch. Von Sophias Wilbur, who won it with 2,273 points. The second

Rottweiler dog in the competition was Ch. Tankerville Digby, who gained a creditable twenty-second place with 805 points.

As we can see, the show scene is quite healthy in South Africa, receiving much sponsorship and assistance. However, the working side is not neglected by any means. South Africa has at the moment six Rottweiler specialist breed clubs, who are affiliated to the Kennel Union of South Africa: one in the Western Cape Province, one in the Eastern Cape Province, one in Durban, Natal and three in the Transvaal Province centred in and around Johannesburg. These breed clubs have regenerated interest in the people who had for some reason left the breed and have now been asked to return to spread their knowledge to the younger members. In working trials, there are a number of dogs who have qualified for CD and CDX, TD1, TD2. There is now a lot of interest in international working trials, which seem to have captured the imagination of the South African Rottweiler owners.

When I last judged in South Africa, I attended a training meeting of the Meridian Rottweiler Club. This was staged in the evening under floodlights on a football pitch. I can truthfully say that there were about a hundred people, male, female, young, old, and of all races, happily

SA Ch. St Tuttson Lando taking the honours from Mr Hondo, a Japanese judge.

training their dogs, all spurred on by the infectious enthusiasm of Dave Lower and the committee of the Meridian Rottweiler Club, who all muck in to help.

It was there that I had the pleasure of meeting Mrs Stella Gawthrop, who has not only the distinction of being a pathfinder for the breed in the UK, but having emigrated to South Africa, has also been of great assistance to the newly formed clubs there. Mrs Gawthrop's first Rottweiler was Adda of Mallion, who held her own at All Breed Shows in the UK; she was placed, which was difficult for a minority breed at the time, in variety classes. Adda was exported to South Africa when her owner emigrated, forming a link between the earliest Rottweilers in the UK and the earliest Rottweilers in South Africa.

The Rottweilers in South Africa now have a very strong breed club system and enthusiastic members. Despite over-breeding and all its knock-on problems, the future of the breed looks very bright.

The Rottweiler in the Caribbean

Barbados

In general, Caribbean countries import from the UK. Barbados has a good show scene with four or five Championship Shows a year. The first two Rottweilers to be imported were a dog known as Herburger Count Nyjinksy and a bitch named Countess Kalinka of Herburger. They were imported by Mrs S. DeGale in 1979.

Once the breed had established itself, many more imports were to follow: Herburger Count Rasputin was imported in 1981 by Mr J. Wilson. Probably the best of the early imports was Hambraugh Perfect Choice, bred by Linda Baughan and imported by Mrs J. Tucker. The next dog of great influence was Adoram Jamie Of Elthor, bred by Michael Quinney and imported by Dr Wayne Welch. The next bitch to be imported was Jagen Blue Moonstone bred by me and imported by Dr Welch. Offspring from this bitch and Jamie were very good, the most notable amongst them was Ch. Elthor Dark Darah, the only champion to have been bred in Barbados to date.

Jamaica

Unlike Barbados, Jamaica holds its own Breed Club Show and specialist judges are invited to officiate.

In 1985, Barbara Butler judged the RAJ Championship Breed Show and her Dog CC was Atlas of Marsden, who was owned by Mr and Mrs E.V. Martin. Best bitch was Sundance Sheezdi Queen. Atlas was Best in Show and the bitch was Best of Opposite Sex.

In May 1986, it was the turn of Joan Clem to officiate. Dog CC went to Ch. Maown Monty of Kenour, who was Reserve Best in Show and Best of Opposite Sex. He was owned by Mr Owen Munroe. Bitch CC and Best in Show went to Ch. Sundance Genevive Hellraiser, who was owned by Winston Tucker.

In 1987, Larry Elsden officiated. Dog CC and Best in Show went to Kenpshot Bandit owned by Robert Bryan. Bitch CC and Reserve Best in Show went to Phillsburgh Ebony, who was owned by Owen Munroe.

In 1988, Mary MacPhail judged the show. Dog CC was given to Ch. Sundance Doctor Bojangles, who was Best of Opposite Sex and was owned by Mrs Andrea Phillips. Bitch CC was Ch. Poirot Vanessa, who was Best in Show. She was owned by Peter Phillips.

In 1989, Ann Garside-Neville judged. Dog CC was given to Cuidado Dirty Harry of Marsden, owned by Vaughn Martin and handled by his UK breeder, Mrs Kate Wood. Best Bitch and Best of Opposite Sex was Ch. Poirot Vanessa, owned by Peter Phillips and Conrodd Chen.

In 1990, the judge was Mrs Pat Price. Her Dog CC and Best in Show was Philsburgh Ezee. Bitch CC and Reserve Best in Show was Ch. Sundance Ballet Princess of Phillsburgh, both owned by R.P. Phillips.

Champions who have been made up in Jamaica give some insight into the breed's development: Chesara Dark Warrior of Copeland, owned by Clyde Fisher; Chesara Lady Macbeth of Copeland, again owned by Clyde Fisher; Attilla Brunhild of Natra, owned by E. Mignott; Chesara Dark Conspirator, owned by D. Walcott; Tasika Angus, owned by D. Judah; Lacie of Copeland, owned by T. Dunn; Carbeth-S Black Concha, owned by W. Evering; Paraiso's Black Caesar, owned by Clyde Fisher; Paraiso's Black Jack, owned by Mr and Mrs M. Fox; Sundance Poirot Northwind, owned by Winston Tucker; Sundance Genevive Hellraiser, owned by Winston Tucker; Sundance Loyal Duchess, owned by Winston Tucker; Maowm Monty of Kemour, owned by Owen Munroe; Sundance Doctor Bojangles of Phillsburgh, owned by Mrs Andrea Phillips; Sundance Baroness, owned by Winston Tucker; Sundance Black Charisma, owned by Mrs C. K. Galma-Tucker; Sundance Ballet Princess of Phillsburgh, owned by Peter Phillips; and Kempshots Drumbeat, owned by Meg Phillips.

During the time we spent in Jamaica, I was greatly impressed with the enthusiasm of the committed Rottweiler owners. Comparing the

Mrs Pat Price judging the Rottweiler Club of Jamaica in 1990.

show scene with that in Barbados, I would say that the fact that there was an established breed club that held its own breed show with specialist judges made all the difference, Barbadian entries being quite small in comparison to the Jamaican ones.

Jamaica is a very cosmopolitan island. The Rottweiler Club of Jamaica in its membership represents almost everyone, cutting across all barriers in a common bond. The happy relaxed atmosphere that Jamaica is famous for was a joy to see.

Trinidad and Tobago

I have never actually visited these islands, but I understand that the Rottweiler presence is quite strong. I have actually exported two dogs to the islands myself, who have become champions: Trinidad and Tobago Ch. Dens Dark Jewel of Jagen, winning at Best in Show level (All Breeds) and Jagen Blue Miami Dolphin, a bitch who gained her title quite quickly. There have been other exports from the UK and Ireland who have done quite well, but news is difficult to come by in spite of many requests for information.

Trin. and Tob. Ch. Densdark Jewel of Jagen, owned by Mr Ferguson.

However, we do know that the first import into Trinidad was Bhaluk Princess Barbella, imported by Mrs Margaret Wattley. This bitch gained her title and also qualified CD. After this bitch, several more imports were made, but, apparently, were quite disappointing.

Unlike the other islands, Trinidad can actually buy from Germany or the USA direct. It has been our experience that Trinidadians love their dogs and a good specimen is highly prized. I am not aware of any breed club in the islands. It is hoped that since the breed is becoming numerically stronger, it will be the next step taken.

2

The Breed Standard

The Federation Cynologique Internationale (FCI) Rottweiler Standard

(Reproduced by kind permission of FCI)

The breed characteristics of the Rottweiler:

General Appearance

Rottweiler breeding aims at a powerful dog, black with well-defined mahogany markings, which despite a massive general appearance is not lacking in nobility and is particularly suitable as a companion, guard dog and working dog.

The Rottweiler is a robust dog, rather above medium size, neither clumsy nor light, neither tall on the leg nor like a greyhound. His frame, which is compact, strong and well proportioned, gives every indication of great strength, agility and endurance. His appearance gives an immediate impression of determination and courage; his demeanour is self-assured, steady and fearless. His calm gaze indicates good humour.

He reacts with great alertness to his surroundings and to his master.

Size: Height at withers:

Dogs	60–68 cm	Bitches	55–63 cm
	60–61 small		55–57 small
	62–64 medium		58–59 medium
	65–66 large		60–61 large
	67–68 very large		62–63 very large

The measurement for the length of the trunk, measured from the breast bone to the point of the rump, should not exceed the height at the withers by more than 15 per cent.

61

Excellent head and outline as demonstrated by Ch. Rottsann Classic Crusader of Vormund, owned by Dunhill.

Head

Of medium length, broad between the ears; the forehead line, seen in profile, moderately arched. The occipital bone is well developed, without protruding too much. The stop and zygomatic arch are well pronounced. The relations of the head are 40 per cent of the total length between bridge of nose and inner eye angle, 60 per cent from inner eye angle to occipital bone.

Scalp   Tightly drawn all over, only forming slight wrinkle when the dog is extremely alert. The aim is head without wrinkles.

Lips   Black, lying close, corners of the mouth closed.

Nose   The bridge of the nose is straight, broad at the root and moderately tapering. Tip of the nose well developed, broad rather than round, with relatively large nostrils and always black in colour.

Eyes   Medium size, almond-shaped and dark brown in colour, with well-fitting eyelids.

A lovely bitch head, neither too strong nor too weak, with the correct ear and eye size.

Ears As small as possible, pendant, triangular, set well apart and high. When the ears are well placed and laid forward the skull appears broader.

Teeth Strong and complete (42 teeth). The upper incisors closing scissor-like over those of the lower jaw.

Neck

Powerful, moderately long, well muscled, with a slightly arched line rising from the shoulders; dry, without dewlap or loose skin on the throat.

Trunk

Roomy, broad and deep chest, with a well-developed forechest and well-sprung ribs. Back straight; powerful and firm. Loins short, powerful and deep. Flanks not drawn up. Croup broad, of medium length and slightly rounded, neither straight nor too sloping.

Tail

Carried horizontally, short and strong. Must be docked if too long at birth.

Forequarters

Shoulders long and well set. The upper arm lies well against the body, but not too tightly. Lower arm strongly developed and muscular. Pasterns slightly springy, strong, not steep. Feet round, very compact and arched. Pads hard, nails short, black and strong. The forelegs, seen from the front, are straight and not set too close together. The lower arms, seen from the side, are straight. The shoulder should have a lay-back of about 45 degrees; the angle between the shoulder blade and the upper arm is about 115 degrees.

Hindquarters

Upper thigh fairly long, broad and well muscled. Lower thigh long, powerful, sinewy, broadly muscled, leading to a powerful hock, well angulated, not steep.

The back feet are somewhat longer than the front feet, equally compact and arched, with strong toes and without dewclaws.

Seen from behind, the back legs are straight and not set too close. In a natural stance, the upper thigh and hip bone, upper thigh and lower thigh, and lower thigh and metatarsus form obtuse angles. The slope of the hip bone is about 20–30 degrees.

Movement

The Rottweiler is a trotter. In this gait, he conveys the impression of strength, endurance and determination. The back stays firm and relatively still. The motion is harmonious, steady, powerful and unhindered, with a good length of stride.

Coat

Consists of outer coat and under coat. The former is bristly, of medium length, coarse, dense and lying close. The under coat must not show through the outer coat. The hair is somewhat longer on both front and hind legs. The colour is black with well-defined markings of a rich, red-brown colour on the cheeks, muzzle, chest and legs, as well as over the eyes and under the tail.

Character

The character of the Rottweiler consists of the sum of all the inherited and acquired physical and mental attributes, qualities and abilities, which determine and regulate his behaviour toward his surroundings.

With regard to his mental make-up, his disposition is basically friendly and peaceful; he is faithful, obedient and willing to work. His temperament, his drive for action and for moving about are moderate. His reaction to disagreeable stimuli is tough, fearless and assured.

His senses are appropriately developed. His reactions are quick and his learning capacity excellent. He is a strong, well-balanced type of dog. Because of his unsuspicious nature, moderate sharpness and high self-confidence, he reacts quietly and without haste to his surroundings. When threatened, however, he goes into action immediately because of his highly developed fighting and protection instincts. Faced with painful experiences, he holds his ground, fearless and

The Rottweiler's disposition is basically friendly and peaceful. He is faithful and obedient.

He does not have a well-developed hunting instinct.

unflinching. When the threat passes, his fighting mood subsides relatively quickly and changes to a peaceful one.

Among his other good qualities are: a strong attachment to his home and a constant readiness to defend it; he is very willing to retrieve and has a good capacity for tracking; he has considerable endurance, likes the water and is fond of children. He does not have a well-developed hunting instinct.

In more detail, the following instincts and character attributes are considered desirable:

In daily life	Self-confidence	High
	Fearlessness	High
	Temperament	Medium
	Endurance	High
	Mobility and Activity	Medium
	Alertness	High
	Tractability	Medium–High
	Mistrust	Low–Medium
	Sharpness	Low–Medium

As companion, guard and working dog

All the qualities described above as well as the following.

Courage	Very High
Fighting Instinct	Very High
Protection Instinct	Very High
Hardness	High

Guarding Characteristics

Watchfulness	Medium
Threshold of Excitability	Medium

Aptitude for nose work

Searching Instinct	Medium
Tracking Instinct	High
Willingness to Retrieve	Medium–High

It should be noted that these instincts and qualities may be present in varying degrees of intensity and that they often merge into one another and are interrelated. They must, however, be present and as highly developed as is necessary for working efficiency.

Appearance and Working Faults

Appearance faults are noticeable deviations from the features described in the Standard. They lessen the working value of the dog only to a limited degree, but they can obscure and distort the typical image of the breed. Appearance faults, according to the Breed Standard, include the following: Light, tall, greyhound-like in general appearance; too long, too short, narrow body; prominent occipital bone; hound-like head and expression; narrow, light, too short, too long, or coarse head; flat forehead (little or no stop); narrow lower jaw; long or pointed muzzle; cheeks too protruding; ram's or split nose, bridge or nose dished or sloping; tip of nose light or spotted; open, pink or spotted lips, corners of the mouth open; distemper teeth; wrinkles on the head; ears set too low, large, long, floppy, turned back, not lying close, or irregularly carried; light (yellow) eyes, or a light and a dark eye, open, deep-set, too full, round, staring eyes, piercing gaze; neck too long, thick, weak muscled, dewlaps or loose skin on throat; forelegs set narrow or not straight; light nails; tail set too high or too low; coat soft, too short or too long, wavy coat, absence of undercoat; markings of the wrong colour, poorly defined or too extensive; white spots; dewclaws on the hind legs.

An otherwise good head spoilt by one ear flying.

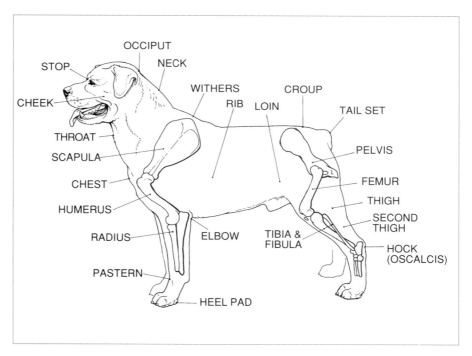

Points of the Rottweiler.

Ear too large and low set.
Too throaty.
Obvious eye problems.

More serious than the faults mentioned previously are those deviations from the ideal which affect both the appearance of the dog and its working qualities. They are called working faults and they are listed in the Standard as follows: Weak bones and musculature; steep shoulders, deficient elbow articulation; too long, too short, or steep upper arm; weak or steep pasterns; splay feet, flat feet or excessively arched toes, stunted toes; flat ribcage, barrel chest, pigeon breast; back too long, weak, sway or roach; croup too short, too straight, too long or too steep; too heavy, unwieldy body; hind legs flatshanked, sickle-hocked, cow-hocked or bow-legged; joints too narrowly or too widely angled.

Excluded from showing and breeding are:

1.   Dogs lacking one or both testicles. Both testicles must be well developed and clearly visible in the scrotum.
2.   All Rottweilers showing an abnormality in the hip joint. The degree of abnormality leading to disqualification and the measures to be taken by breeders, are set forth by the Breeding Committee.
3.   All Rottweilers with faulty bites and dentition, ie overshot, under-

69

Weak pasterns.

shot and missing premolars or molars. (X-rays are not accepted as proof of complete dentition).

4.   All Rottweilers with loose or rolled-in eyelids (entropion), as well as those with open eyelids (ectropion). In case of doubt, veterinary examination is recommended when a dog with eye trouble is presented at a breed show or breeding eligibility test. The judge is responsible for sending information about the dog in question to the Studbook Office. If the trouble is still present when the dog is shown again, or if the eyelids have been operated on, the dog is forever banned from breeding. Concealment of an eye operation is one of the worst deceptions and according to the show rules is to be prosecuted as a breeding violation.

5.   All Rottweilers with yellow eyes, hawk eyes, staring expression or with eyes of different colours.

6.   All Rottweilers with pronounced reversal of sexual characteristics (bitchy dogs, doggy bitches).

7.   All timid, cowardly, gunshy, vicious, excessively mistrustful and nervous Rottweilers, as well as those of stupid expression and behaviour. Dogs which show obvious laziness, unusually slow reactions or extreme one-sidedness in their character should be watched and ex-

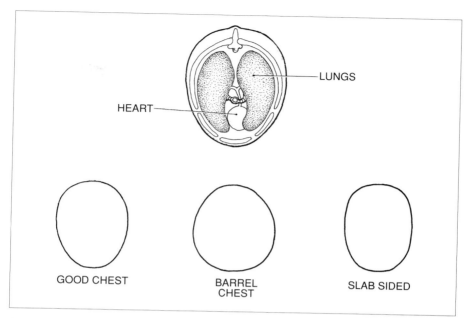

Cross-section of chest.

Dipping topline. Lacks depth. Long in hock. Boxy head.

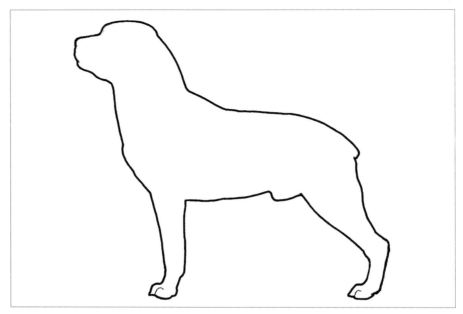

Sloping off at croup. Sickle-hocked.

Steep upper arm, straight stifles, lacks second thigh.

Weak pasterns, incorrect tail set.

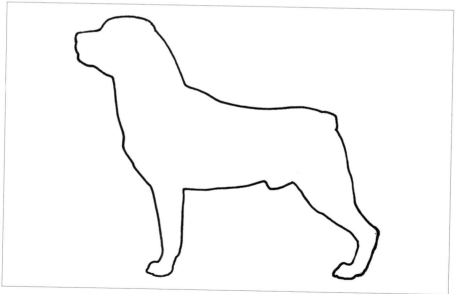

Dipping topline, sickle hocked, short in leg.

amined with particular care before they are used for breeding (the possibility of deafness should be considered).

8. Decidedly long-coated or wavy-coated Rottweilers. Smooth-coated or short-coated dogs with an absence of undercoat should be used for breeding only with the permission of the chief breed warden.

The Teeth

The adult dog has 42 teeth; 12 incisors, 4 fangs or corner teeth, 16 premolars and 10 molars. The teeth are of extremely vital importance to the dog. No Rottweiler will be judged or used for breeding who does not have a well-formed, correct and complete set of teeth.

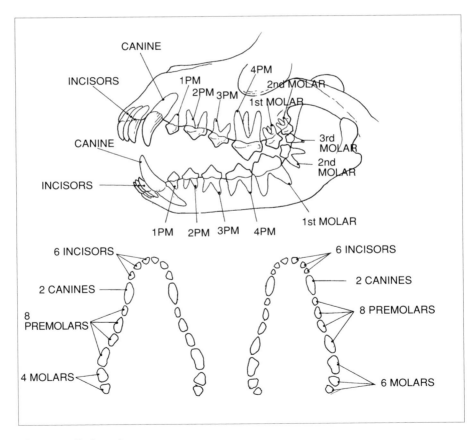

The Rottweiler's teeth.

With very few exceptions, depending on the shape of the dog's head, all should have the so-called 'scissor-bite'. It is the natural, regular set of teeth, which all dogs have, whereby the upper incisors seize – slightly grinding – a little bit over the lower ones. If this grinding touch is missing, there will be a clear space between the incisors of the upper jaw and those of the lower jaw. This is called an overbite. If the teeth of the lower jaw are in front of those of the upper jaw, one considers it an underbite. Both forms are defects and result in disqualification of the dog. A set of teeth like pincers, biting upon one another, i.e. both rows of the incisors touching each other directly, is still admissible. However, it usually degrades the dog and puts him one class lower when he is judged.

Running Gear and Gaits

The hindquarters are the means of support and act as a leverage for locomotion. In every type of action the forward thrust proceeds from the hindquarters, which are more strongly angulated and have more

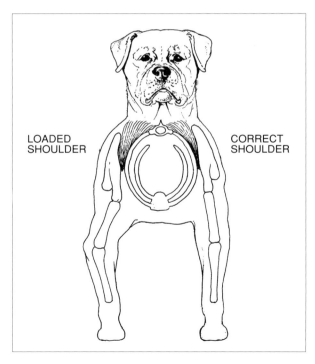

LOADED SHOULDER

CORRECT SHOULDER

A loaded shoulder. Incorrect exercise can thicken muscles under the shoulder blade, forcing it outwards. This in turn will push out the elbow.

powerful and complex muscles than the forequarters. In conformity with the greater strain placed on them, the forequarters show a less angled system for support and braking. The propulsive forces are transmitted to the forequarters through the trunk. The back plays an essential part in the forward movement, the powerful extensor muscles of the neck and back co-operating with the lower neck muscles, as well as with those of the inside thigh and stomach. Extremely strong and well-developed back muscles are essential for a good and enduring gait.

The types of gait in the Rottweiler are the walk, the trot, the pace, the gallop and the leap.

In the trot, the forequarters and hindquarters are mutually synchronized (brace, lift, float, support). The back remains relatively stable.

In the walk, the back movements are more visible; in the pace (simultaneous advance of the hind and front limbs on one side), they are more pronounced and strongest of all in the gallop, when the back is arched like a spring and throws the body forward.

Faulty types of gait are: stiff, constrained, too high or dragging the ground, short steps, rocking, swaying, rolling, weaving.

General Comments on External Appearance

Defects in harmony (balance) and soundness of the body structure detract from the dog's appearance and working ability.

A dog's working usefulness depends essentially on his ability to move and run, and these factors, therefore, receive particular attention in assessing the appearance and character. There are several references in the Standard to the importance of the length and power of the limbs, the back and shoulders, the angulation of the joints and the muscles.

In judging a living thing, other imponderables also come into play, which only the trained eye of an experienced judge can correctly assess within the framework of the total picture.

A few figures may be mentioned for guidance: A Rottweiler, which is 65cm at the withers, should measure about 75cm from the breast bone to the point of rump. The chest circumference should be about equal to the height at the withers, plus 20cm. The chest depth should be neither more, nor very much less, than 50 per cent of the height of the withers.

The USA Breed Standard

(Reproduced by kind permission of the American Kennel Club)

General Appearance

The ideal Rottweiler is a medium large, robust and powerful dog, black with clearly defined rust markings. His compact and substantial build denotes great strength, agility and endurance. Dogs are characteristically more massive throughout with larger frame and heavier bone than bitches. Bitches are distinctly feminine, but without weakness of substance or structure.

Size, Proportion, Substance

Dogs: 24in to 27in. Bitches: 22in to 25in with preferred size being mid-range of each sex. Correct proportion is of primary importance, as long as size is within the Standard's range. The length of body, from prosternum to the rear-most projection of the rump, is slightly longer than the height of the dog at the withers. The most desirable proportion of height to length being 9 to 10. The Rottweiler is neither coarse nor shelly. Depth of chest is approximately fifty per cent (50%) of the height of the dog. His bone and muscle mass must be sufficient to balance his frame, giving a compact and very powerful appearance.

Serious Faults   Lack of proportion, undersize, reversal of sex characteristics (bitchy dogs, doggy bitches).

Head

Of medium length, broad between the ears; forehead line seen in profile is moderately arched; zygomatic arch and stop well developed with strong, broad upper and lower jaws. The desired ratio of skull to muzzle is 3 to 2. Skull is preferred dry, however some wrinkling may occur when dog is alert. Expression is noble, alert and self-assured.

77

Eyes

Eyes are of medium size, almond-shaped with well fitting lids, moderately deep set, neither protruding nor receding. The desired colour is a uniform dark brown.

Serious Faults   Yellow (bird of prey) eyes, eyes of different colour or size, hairless eye rim.

Ears

Ears of medium size, pendant, triangular in shape; when carried alertly the ears are level with the top of the skull and appear to broaden it. Ears are to be set well apart, hanging forward with the inner edge lying tightly against the head and terminating at approximately mid-cheek.

Serious Faults Improper carriage (creased, folded or held away from cheek/head).

Muzzle

Bridge is straight, broad at base with slight tapering towards tip. The end of the muzzle is broad with well developed chin. Nose is large and always black. Lips always black; corners closed; inner mouth pigment is preferred dark.

Serious Faults   Lack of pigment (pink mouth).

Bite and Dentition

Teeth 42 in number (20 upper, 22 lower), strong correctly placed, meeting in a scissors bite – lower incisors touching inside of upper incisors.

Serious Faults   Level bite, any missing tooth.

Disqualification   Overshot, undershot (when incisors do not touch or mesh); markedly wry mouth; 2 or more missing teeth.

Neck, Topline, Body

Neck   Powerful, well muscled, moderately long, slightly arched and without loose skin.

Topline   The back is firm and level, extending in a straight line from behind the withers to the croup. The back remains horizontal to the ground while the dog is moving or standing.

Body   The chest is roomy, broad and deep, reaching to elbow, with well-pronounced forechest and well-sprung, oval ribs. Back is straight and strong; loin is short, deep and well muscled; croup is broad, of medium length and only slightly sloping. Underline of a mature Rottweiler has no distinct tuck-up. Tail docked short, close to body. The set of the tail is more important than length. Properly set, it gives an impression of elongation of topline; carried slightly above horizontal when the dog is excited or moving.

Forequarters

Shoulder blade is long and well laid back. Upper arm equal in length to shoulder blade, set so elbows are well under body. Distance from withers to elbow and elbow to ground is equal. Legs are strongly developed with straight, heavy bone, not set close together. Pasterns are strong, springy and almost perpendicular to ground. Feet are round, compact with well-arched toes, turning neither in nor out. Pads are thick and hard. Nails short, strong and black. Dewclaws may be removed.

Hindquarters

Angulation of hindquarters balances that of forequarters. Upper thigh is fairly long, very broad and well muscled. Stifle joint is well turned. Lower thigh is long, broad and powerful with extensive muscling leading into a strong hock joint. Rear pasterns are relatively short in length and nearly perpendicular to the ground. Viewed from the rear, hindlegs are straight, strong and wide enough apart to fit with a properly built body. Feet are somewhat longer than front feet, turning neither in nor out, equally compact with well arched toes. Pads are thick and hard. Nails short, strong and black. Dewclaws must be removed.

Coat

Outer coat is straight, coarse, dense, of medium length and lying flat. Undercoat must be present on neck and thighs, but is not to show through outer coat. Amount of undercoat is influenced by climatic conditions. The coat is shortest on head, ears and legs, longest on breeching. The Rottweiler is to be exhibited in a natural condition with no trimming.

Fault   Wavy coat.

Serious Faults   Open, excessively short or curly coat; total lack of undercoat; any trimming that alters the length of the natural coat.

Disqualification   Long coat.

Colour and Markings

Always black with rust to mahogany markings. The demarcation between black and rust is to be clearly defined. The markings should be located as follows: a spot over each eye; on cheeks; as a strip around each side of muzzle, but not on the bridge of the nose; on throat; triangular mark on either side of prosternum; on forelegs from carpus downwards to toes; on front of rear legs from hock to toes, but not completely eliminating black from back of rear pasterns; under tail; black penciling on toes. The undercoat is grey or black. Quantity and location of rust markings is important and should not exceed ten per cent of body colour.

Serious Faults   Straw-coloured, excessive, insufficient or sooty markings; rust marking other than described above; white marking any place on dog (a few rust or white hairs do not constitute a marking).

Disqualifications   Any base colour other than black; absence of all markings.

Gait

The Rottweiler is a trotter. His movement should be balanced, harmonious, sure, powerful and unhindered, with strong fore-reach and a powerful rear drive. The motion is effortless, efficient and ground covering. Front and rear legs are thrown neither in nor out, as the imprint of hind feet should touch that of forefeet. In a trot the forequarters and hindquarters are mutually co-ordinated while the back remains level, firm and relatively motionless. As speed increases, the legs will converge under the body towards a centre line.

Temperament

The Rottweiler is basically a calm, confident and courageous dog with a self-assured aloofness that does not lend itself to immediate and indiscriminate friendships. With little suspicion and high self-confidence, the Rottweiler responds quietly and with a wait-and-see attitude to influences in his environment. He has an inherent desire to protect home and family and is an intelligent dog of extreme hardness and adaptability, with a strong willingness to work, making him especially suited as a companion, guardian and general all-purpose dog. The behaviour of the Rottweiler in the show ring should be controlled, willing and adaptable, trained to submit to examination of mouth, testicles etc. An aloof or reserved dog should not be penalized, as this reflects the accepted character of the breed. An aggressive or belligerent attitude towards other dogs should not be faulted.

Faults

The foregoing is a description of the ideal Rottweiler. Any structural fault that detracts from the above described working dog must be penalized to the extent of the deviation.

Disqualifications

Overshot or undershot (where incisors do not touch or mesh); markedly wry mouth; 2 or more missing teeth; long coat; any base colour other than black; absence of all markings.

3

Buying your Puppy

Buying your puppy is probably the most important decision you will make concerning your dog. It is amazing how little thought goes into this.

Why a Rottweiler?

It is important to ask yourself why you want a Rottweiler. Is it really the breed for you?

Ch. Jagen Blue Trigo, owned by Broom and Rutherford.

A Rottweiler doing the job he was once bred for.

The Rottweiler is very adaptable. One bitch we bred, Champion Jagen Blue Trigo, did the original job she was bred for for many years. Owned by Jo Rutherford, Trigo rounded up the milking herd and brought it back to the milking parlour in Devon. In Vienna, a Rottweiler was awarded the title King of the Guide Dogs.

I have seen Rottweilers retrieving game, rescuing people buried under snow, working for the army, rescuing people from the water. Trials dogs, Schutzhund dogs, agility competitors, pulling carts or sledges; the list is impressive. What a Rottweiler is not is a dog you can keep shut up for twenty-three hours a day. He is content when he is working, because when he is working he is pleasing his owner and that is what a Rottweiler really loves to do. He is happiest when he is with his master or mistress. To be left alone on a chain is heartbreaking, literally. So whatever the reasons you choose this breed, his intelligence and exercise requirement must be borne in mind.

Dog or Bitch?

Having decided that a Rottweiler is for you, you must then decide whether to have a dog or a bitch. I always advise people to have a bitch if it is their first Rottweiler. I must admit to preferring bitches myself, although I can see the appeal of a dog. Bitches are easier to live with, except for when they come into season, which must be endured. They are not arrogant, yet can guard every bit as well as a male. A bitch will enjoy a cuddle, whereas a dog will pretend not to enjoy love, even when you can tell he does, and I generally find that bitches make more loyal companions.

Breeding

Very good bitches can be bred from. Only excellent dogs may be used at stud. If you intend to build up a show kennel, a very good quality bitch is your first priority. You can always use the best stud available. It is very rare that you can buy a dog good enough to used at stud. It requires a solid apprenticeship in the breed before you are able to cope with the responsibility of stud dog ownership.

Why a Puppy?

Some people do not like the puppy stage and go for an older dog or bitch. There is always a risk with a second-hand dog, although hundreds of Rottweilers have been rehoused successfully in the UK by the Rottweiler rescue scheme. A registered charity, all dogs and prospective owners are vetted and this accounts for the high success rate but it must be kept in mind that people who need to find a new home for their dog usually have a problem, or a problem dog. Be careful: it may be a problem passed on to you.

Choosing the Right Puppy

So often, I have watched people pick over one of our litters, sometimes nervous or apologetic for taking so long. I tell them to take their time; it is hoped that the dog will be with them for the next ten years or more – what are a few minutes? If you need help, just ask. It is extremely important to go to an experienced breeder with a proven track record;

Typical outgoing six-week-old puppies.

he will have seen the litter every day and will know each pup's individual character, faults and virtues.

In truth, most good breeders have already graded the litter time and time again, long before you arrive. You may want a show prospect, an obedience or trials dog, or just a pet. First choice of a litter may depend on what you require of your acquisition. The breeder is best placed to advise you. If you do not trust your breeder of his choice, re-examine why you have gone to this particular person in the first place. Perhaps a look elsewhere would be in order. It is important to be able to relax and feel comfortable. If you are on edge, perhaps you are being pushed into something you might regret.

To arrive at your choice of breeder, you have started gathering information months, perhaps years beforehand. A study of showing form, or one particular individual may draw you to a particular breeder's kennel. Perhaps consistent wins in the obedience ring or in trials by a breeder's dogs inspires you to want to own a great working dog; or perhaps the reason is just recommendation from a trusted friend.

Whatever the reason, let it be a good one. So often I hear of people who see an advertisement in the local press, go that very evening and purchase purely on impulse. This, I am afraid to say, often leads to disappointment. By sunrise, one or two members of the family, having slept on it, start to think, 'but I wanted to show', or 'I wanted to work our new dog' and on reading the pup's ancestry find no track record for either. So the most important factor is, of course, that a dog is a sound family friend and companion, but having said that, why limit your aspirations?

The following is a check-list for prospective puppy buyers:

1.   Have the parents been X-rayed for hip dysplasia and do they hold eye certificates?
2.   Have the parents been through an approved character test?
3.   Can you meet and handle the pup's mother?
4.   Does the breeder replace the pup free-of-charge if it is found to suffer from any hereditary fault?
5.   Does the breeder give a full back-up service, with practical help and advice?
6.   Have the parents been shown? If so, what awards were achieved? Are they champions?
7.   Have the parents any working qualifications?

Points 1–5 are imperative; gold stars for 6 and 7.

It is impossible to detail every virtue or fault you should look for when making your choice, but here I list a few pointers which may help.

Check the teeth. When closed together, the top set of teeth should be just in front of the bottom set. This is known as a scissor-bite and is discussed in more detail on page 74.

The eyes will not yet have their permanent colour, but pale grey eyes will not often turn yellow, so choose the darkest.

The ears should be neat and in proportion to the head. Puppies do not grow into very large ears, as some people try to tell you.

The neck should never be too short or stuffy.

The body is cobby at this stage. Pups tend to lengthen in body as they grow. Correct proportions are as 9 is to 10 (height to length).

A well-socialized Rottweiler.

Check the legs and feet. A well-reared puppy should have a fair amount of bone and a strong, straight front, that is the forelegs should appear parallel when viewed from the front, the feet turning neither in nor out (a certain allowance may be made for puppyish softness). The feet should be tight and never splayed.

Movement is always hard to assess at this age, but avoid any puppy who moves erratically or is obviously lame!

Examine the coat. At eight weeks, most pups have a soft coat. Look out for overlong coats or wavy coats. Actual long coats, although difficult to spot at this age, will show in fluffy long hairs on the ears in particular. A good, rich, well-defined tan is desired. Discard light, over-marked or very dark colours.

Assess temperament. Puppies should always be outgoing. Avoid shy puppies.

These tips are intended to help, but should not be regarded as foolproof. Many swans turn to geese and vice versa!

Having made your choice, it is time to take your puppy home. As a breeder, I give one week's supply of food with each puppy. If your breeder does not do this, ask if you can buy some food that the pup is used to. The puppy will be stressed enough without a change of diet to contend with.

Insurance should be arranged as soon as possible. The first six months are the most dangerous and can be very expensive. Insure against veterinary fees and loss and, of course, third party liability.

The first night home is the worst. Your puppy is tense and will more often than not cry after being taken from his litter-mates. A warm bed and an alarm clock for company often work since it is said that the clock's ticking sounds like mother's heartbeat. Do not give in and take your puppy to bed with you; rather, invest in some cotton wool for your ears!

It is important that dogs do not become accustomed to sleeping in your bedroom. This is your inner sanctum, in basic dog psychology. The dog will feel that he has taken one step up the ladder if he is allowed into your sleeping quarters. It is a fact that most people bitten for the first time by their own dog are bitten in the bedroom. In our breed, it is important to treat dogs as dogs. I do not mean you should love them any less, but discipline is very important and must be started from the outset.

4
Development and Training

The bond between man and dog goes back ten thousand years. The dog has a special relationship with man and is described as his best friend. But sometimes, this friendship breaks down, usually through the stupidity of the human partner. Dogs in general, Rottweilers in particular, are loyal and reliable; dare I say, much more reliable than human beings! We have taken from the Rottweiler, companionship and help in many fields: hunting, protecting our homes and family, pulling carts, acting as guide dogs for the blind, search and rescue, herding cattle and so on. In return, we give our companion shelter and food. It is an unwritten agreement and if we renege on it, let us not be surprised if our dog loses his respect for us, for we are not worthy of being called Master.

In modern times, the demands we make have changed in some ways. The tasks we had set the Rottweiler have become lost and very rarely will you find a Rottweiler today herding cattle anywhere in the world, although most could still accomplish this task if required. The majority of Rottweilers are kept as pets: this is a pigeon-hole Rottweilers do not fit into with ease; there has to be something else. Some people show their dogs, some work them. Whatever you do, it is as well to remember our half of the bargain; a Rottweiler is far too intelligent to be left in a kennel for twenty-three hours a day.

Rottweilers as a breed need some activity or work if they are not to become bored and frustrated. The form this takes depends entirely on the circumstances of the owner. People who show their dogs expose them to many new forms of stimuli. The dog is with his owner for the greater part of the weekend and, through the week, the dog is road walked to produce fitness and show condition, so the ordinary show dog, apart from receiving the care and love of his owner, receives exercise and mental stimulus and is bonded with his owner by a common purpose. Much in the same way, although on a higher level, the obedience competitors, in which I include trials and Schutzhund workers, train their dogs throughout the week and aim either to win a qualification or pass a test. Again, man and dogs are bonded by the same purpose. The end result is that both dog and owner gain satisfaction and a richer existence. Even the most beautiful house and garden can become a prison. A Rottweiler needs more than this; he must have some purpose. Having said that, each and every Rottweiler who is taken out into the public's glare is an ambassador for the breed and we must do the best we can.

Jealousy and Fighting

It is not uncommon to find households with two or more Rottweilers and it is in these situations, that sometimes, the green-eyed monster can appear. This usually happens when the pecking order in the pack is upset, or a new arrival causes confusion to the status quo. One theory is that you should dominate the dog who is lowest in the pecking order to make him realize that he is the lowest and to prevent problems from occurring. However, I feel it is better to dominate all dogs equally and make them come to a submissive position in front of the owner, preferably the down position. By reinforcing your own dominance, you may well steal the thunder of the antagonists.

I have always found Rottweiler bitches to be worse than dogs in this respect. The presence of one antagonistic bitch turned our kennels into a constant battleground and caused resentment which was too deep to heal. So, for many years, we just had to learn to live with it and all our bitches were walked individually.

Dogs will respect an older dog or bitch. I have seen our old matriarch walk between two younger antagonists and break up a fight with a snarl, even though she was aged and barely able to walk. The respect the younger dogs showed this bitch was quite amazing. I have been told by many other breeders that they have experienced a similar thing in their own kennels and so we can assume that the pecking order is not always maintained through physical strength. Age and experience also command great respect.

Fights between dogs can start over the smallest thing. I once heard of a case where two dogs fought almost to the death over an empty sweet paper. It is essential that the owner is pack leader at all times and that the dog is affectionately subordinate. Disobedient dogs must be disciplined consistently by voice command and direct stare. When you show disapproval to a dog, reinforce this by ignoring him for a time. Do not scold and then pet a short time later as this will only confuse him.

The Character of the Rottweiler

To define Rottweiler character, we must look back to the breed's history. The Rottweiler is a working dog, a cattle dog. He exhibits protecting and guarding qualities and for many years has been used as a Schutzhund sport dog. We have all seen, in the Breed Standards, certain definitions of what is required of Rottweiler character: self-confidence – high; fearlessness – high; sharpness – medium/low; fighting instinct – high; defensive instinct – very high; hardness – high, tractability – medium.

Self-Confidence

Self-confidence describes the dog's ability to act on his own initiative and to face stressful situations without becoming fearful. The term that comes to mind and is much used by Germans in the training clubs is 'empty vessels make the most noise'. In other words, a dog who continually barks and shows fear can never be regarded as a dog with high self-confidence. A dog who has high self-confidence is never worried by strangers or strange stimuli. He is totally aware that he is able to cope with every situation. He will look you squarely in the eye, with a steady gaze. If you suddenly raised your arm to scratch your head, he would not duck. He is not afraid because you represent no threat to him. Having said this, there is a great difference between a dog with high self-confidence and a gentle, phlegmatic one. The former will always appear arrogant, while the latter will seek appeasement.

Fearlessness

Fearlessness is self-explanatory and is demonstrated by the dog's tolerance of unusual or disagreeable stimuli. Fear is an emotional state of mind, caused by a sense of impending danger or pain. So fearlessness and self-confidence have a very narrow dividing line and in some respects are the same.

Sharpness

Sharpness describes a dog's reaction to hostility or unfriendly approach. Perhaps this is the biggest bone of contention in our modern-day evaluation of the Rottweiler. Whereas the pet Rottweiler living at home would require a low degree of sharpness, a Schutzhund dog or a dog who is required to guard a family home would need to have at least a medium degree of sharpness. What we most certainly do not want is a dog with high fearlessness and high sharpness. This would be a very dangerous dog in a non-working environment. Sharpness can be learned in training and can also be inherited. The Rottweiler with a naturally high degree of sharpness, without any form of training should be considered undesirable.

Fighting Instinct

The Rottweiler's fighting instinct is high. It is mainly inherited, although it can be learned at a very early age in the nest. Fighting instinct has a direct parallel with play instinct and in puppies can be observed as being one and the same. Play instinct is redirected into working ability and willingness to perform tasks. In Schutzhund work, fighting instinct and play are used to teach the dog to take the sleeve. As I have said before, there is no animosity between the dog and the helper. It is a trick he has been taught and he enjoys doing it. If the sleeve is released and dropped on the floor, the dog will pick it up and run round shaking it in a play-type mode.

Defensive Instinct

A dog's defensive instinct is his need to protect himself and the other members of his pack, which in these days usually includes the family unit. In the Rottweiler, this instinct is very high and can be developed by training, quite easily unfortunately. Many Rottweilers have been encouraged forward at an early age by less than proficient trainers, who then find that the dog's defensive instinct matures, they are powerless to control the fruit of their labour. Many Rottweilers are thought to be too soft when young and encouraged forward, forward, forward, in their defensive instinct. A six-month-old Rottweiler dog may appear quite a large dog in size, but mentally he is still very much a baby. The defensive instinct must be allowed to mature slowly, like a good wine. So many good young dogs have been ruined at an early age by incompetent trainers.

Hardness

A hard Rottweiler is one who does not allow bad experiences to affect him permanently. If one were to step backwards onto a hard dog's foot, the dog may give out a yelp but will return immediately to the handler, who, it is hoped, would bend down and apologize for his action. A soft dog would cower, perhaps holding his foot up to let you know that he has been hurt and even if you move towards him to apologize, he will move away with a worried expression. It is only if you kneel down and call him to you that will he come slowly for his apology. A hard dog will usually have forgotten the experience by now and will be back at heel.

Tractability (or Biddability)

A Rottweiler who is both biddable and hard will have the true Rottweiler character. It is this wonderful mix that makes the Rottweiler so unique. I think many people who have tried to analyse Rottweiler characters have not realized how much this unique mix plays a part.

Ch. Jagen Blue Aria.

Stages of Development

The temperament we look for in our dog primarily depends on the work or function assigned to him. To say that temperament is to a certain degree putty in the owner's hands, is fair comment. The temperament of a dog is partly inherited and partly moulded by environmental aspects. The inherited traits can be suppressed because a puppy is born with a brain that is not fully developed. Much of the development takes place after birth, so the young puppy requires an environment with stimulating surroundings.

Up to Three Weeks

The puppy is born blind; it sleeps and eats a great deal, gradually building up its size and strength. It is important that the dam is kept as quiet a possible - a relaxed mother has contented pups. Do not bring the neighbours and family around to see the newborns, as this will only induce stress in the dam which will be passed to the pups. It can also cause a reduced milk yield, thus making the pups cry, creating yet more stress.

Two-day-old pups, rounded and content.

Four to Eight Weeks

The puppy can now see and identifies its environment: dam, breeder, food and litter-mates. This is a very important stage in the development of a Rottweiler and the breeder can make or break a puppy at this stage. His influence is vital. Mistakes made now cannot be rectified later in life. It is important for the breeder to handle the puppies carefully at least once a day, in order to establish human contact. The hands of a human should make the puppy feel warm and reassured. Later in life, hands will give praise, love and food.

Eight to Twelve Weeks

The puppy will now be in his new home. He will learn very quickly after the first stressful period when he leaves his litter-mates. House-training and primary obedience can start now. This is the period when the new owner asserts himself as pack leader. Lots of affection and praise should be given when the pup is good, or performs a new task successfully.

Twelve to Seventeen Weeks

This stage is similar to the last, but the puppy is stronger and growing fast. Rottweilers need plenty of new stimuli: rides in the car and very short walks outside the home environment. Play is very important but, with a strong, guarding breed, the play must be controlled. The owner must firmly, but gently, win all the games. In this way, he confirms his pack leadership. In the same way, the rest of the family must be equally firm, thus establishing the pecking order. The puppy must be on the lowest level. Once this is established, he is quite happy. Never feed the puppy before the family – this way he understands he is last in the pecking order.

Six to Twelve Months

This stage can be difficult, in the same way that teenagers are difficult for human parents. It is important to keep calm and firmly reinforce the lessons already learnt. I am not against physical punishment if it is needed, but only if it is called for. Sometimes a puppy will aggressively resist our demands, or ignore us completely. The first deserves a whack, the second does not. You cannot blame the puppy if you are being boring! If you decide to whack, you must always finish up being the dominant one - do not hit and run. The puppy must be held down until it stops growling or acting aggressively. You must put a growl in your own voice when reprimanding the pup, while holding the loose skin on the neck. It will be observed that this is the way its own mother asserts her dominance and will easily be understood by the pup.

Twelve Months to Two Years

In this period, the Rottweiler attains his sexual maturity and guarding instinct. His home and garden is patrolled, without command. It always seems funny when a Rottweiler guards for the first time, barking loudly, usually backing off, not quite sure if he is doing the right thing. When dogs bark, it is a call for assistance, calling up the pack if you like. A barking dog is not usually dangerous. If you see a dog make a controlled attack in a Schutzhund test, that attack is always silent, except when he is holding the helper at bay in the hide, when he again calls up the pack (his handler). So when your youngster barks and looks back at you, reassure him with a pat. If it is the postman, introduce them; let him know this man represents no threat.

The Adult Dog

Your puppy is now a young mature adult and let us assume he has gone through puppyhood with no problems. Even at this stage, he can develop new behaviour patterns, which we may consider undesirable. He must be prepared to curtail this new behaviour before it becomes a habit.

The basic principles of correction and praise apply not only to the well-balanced puppy, but also to the adult dog who has been acquired second-hand. With a large dog, like a Rottweiler, it may be beyond the capability of the new owner to dominate the newly acquired adult dog. In such cases, I would recommend that you seek professional help, for the dog you have acquired may have already been in conflict with his former family and won the contest. Such dogs do not take well to a lower pecking order and skilful training is necessary.

Any Rottweiler that makes an unprovoked attack on a human being should be destroyed. Here in the UK, we have to clean up the image of our Rottweilers, which has been so tarnished in recent years. We cannot afford any more incidents. In the same way, any dog who will not accept dominance in his new pack is not an asset to anyone. He is a liability, not only to the family, but also to the breed.

Old Age

The life expectancy of a Rottweiler varies from ten to fifteen years, and, in the main, bitches tend to live longer than dogs. Older Rottweilers have special needs. They need somewhere warm and soft to sleep and the bed should be made twice as thick as it is normally. Old Rottweilers may need to be let out more frequently to answer the call of nature, but for shorter periods. Older Rottweilers tend to drink more and sleep more.

People often worry about introducing a puppy into a home where there is already an aged Rottweiler, feeling that this will upset or unsettle the older dog. I have found quite the opposite to be true. The puppy often gives the older dog a new lease of life. The single dog, who has probably been bored for many years, suddenly has a new playmate, who like himself, sleeps most of the time, but will enjoy a game for short periods. The older dog also teaches the younger puppy good habits and the puppy will often watch and copy the older dog's actions. It is wonderful to see. And when that dreadful day comes when the old-timer leaves you forever, that parting may not be so painful.

Old-timers can teach a lot to young pups.

97

Psychology of Training

Correction-Praise

The first common mistake people make is to imagine that a dog thinks in the same way as a human being. Dogs do not reason; they learn mainly by association. Training by association or 'correction-praise' works on the principle that a dog is motivated by knowing that a good action is followed by pleasure and reward and a bad action is followed by correction. If we command our dog to sit and he responds, we then pat him and tell him what a good boy he is. Very basic. The dog knows that if he obeys our command, he will be rewarded by pleasure.

It is an extremely good method of training but, to be effective, the praise or correction must be given immediately. There is no point in correcting a dog even thirty seconds after he has committed the misdemeanour. It must be done at the time. Many a good dog has been ruined when he has done something good and, for some reason, not received the right response from the handler; in other words, the wrong association has been created. It is a long haul back to the beginning.

Reward is often denied by people who train by correction only: the dog is commanded to sit and, if he does not respond, he receives a whack and is pushed into position. In the dog's mind, the association is purely negative: 'If I don't sit, I receive a whack'.

The correction-praise method illicits a far better response. The dog is commanded to sit and if he doesn't do it the first time, he is pushed gently into position. When in position, he is lovingly praised.

The most common example of correction-praise going wrong is where a dog runs off and refuses to come back, either rabbiting or playing with other dogs. The owner pursues the dog and eventually catches him. The angry owner then proceeds to whack the dog, thus reinforcing the idea that if the dog comes back, he receives a whack, which is totally opposite to what the owner is trying to achieve. The ideal thing to do in such a situation is to praise the dog lavishly when he is caught even though deep in your heart you would like to strangle him!

Often, dogs that run off and stay just out of distance can be discouraged from this habit when the owner hides. The dog looks back to see where the owner is, panics at being unable to see him and comes running back. As he runs back, the owner shows himself. The dog will always run to the owner to be reassured. Lavish praise should then be heaped on the dog and the dog be allowed to go again. Do not immediately put him on the lead, for this will reinforce the idea that when he comes back to you, he is immediately going to be taken home and, in future, will associate coming to you with the end of the walk or game.

The Owner's Example

Many owners do not realize what effect their own behaviour has on their dog. A dog is a pack animal and will pick up pack instincts. Some behaviour patterns are learned. For instance, horses in a field on the side of a road will totally ignore traffic rushing by because the older horses show no fear and just continue grazing. The youngsters learn that there is nothing to fear and, after a time, they also totally ignore the traffic noise. But, say a wolf or a lion entered the field. The older horses would immediately thunder off in the opposite direction and the youngsters would immediately follow. In this way, youngsters learn what is dangerous and what is not to be feared.

In the same way, the owner of a dog can pass on his own phobias. Let us assume a situation where the owner has a fear of low-flying aircraft. If the young adult dog or puppy sees the owner run screaming to the

Good companions. Both these dogs had been re-homed, and are now firm friends.

house in terror, it is not unreasonable to assume that the dog will quickly follow. As I have said before, the dog is a pack animal and so much of his learning comes through conditioning. He sees that his pack leader is terrified by the aeroplane and so he, being on a lower level, will accept that this aeroplane represents a real danger. Therefore, when the next plane arrives, he will also show signs of tension, stress and fear.

Reverse Training

Some annoying habits, like jumping up, can be reversed. The puppy was probably encouraged to jump up when he was small and everyone thought it was quite fun, but now he is large, and has probably just come in from a swim in the pool and Aunty is standing there in her Sunday best. The best-turned out person in the world can be quickly reduced to tramp-like condition by a muddy Rottweiler.

The way to reverse this habit is to have the dog on a check chain and lead. One person holds the lead and stands behind the dog who is sitting. Another person approaches and encourages the dog to jump up. As the dog does so, he is taken down by a snatch on the lead. The process is then repeated with another person approaching, who also encourages the dog to jump up. Again, he is taken down by a very firm snatch of the lead. It is rare for a dog to jump up on the third occasion. However, to maintain this amended behaviour pattern, it may be necessary to repeat this training once or twice a week to ensure that it is permanently reinforced.

As you can see, for every problem or bad habit, there is usually someone who knows a foolproof solution. If you have a problem and you are getting nowhere yourself, do not continue to struggle on alone, but seek advice, either from a training club or from a Rottweiler club. They are there to help you and their experience is there to be tapped.

Keeping the Dog's Interest

A dog must enjoy working. When I say working, I include just every-day general obedience, for I class this as working every bit as much as training dogs up to very high Schutzhund standard. Most dogs will be motivated by praise and will therefore enjoy training sessions. It is clear to see at most training clubs that praise is in very short supply with novice and even more experienced handlers. Some people train by correction only. This kind of training never has long lasting results, only very unhappy dogs. At the end of every exercise, praise your dog. It doesn't cost anything.

In the years I have trained Rottweilers, I have always found there to be a barrier at a certain stage where the dog becomes stubborn. If you tell him to jump a jump twice, he does it; but when you tell him to jump it a third time, he says, 'I've had it, I've done it twice and I'm not going to do it again!' It is extremely important that you do not give up at this point and this is where training really begins. He is made to jump it a third time, even if you have to stand there all night. The dog must not be allowed to win.

I am only using jumping as an example. It applies to all things. Some Rottweilers, having done heel work for five minutes, will sit down and refuse to go any more. Unless there is an injury or an hereditary problem, there is no excuse for it and I must admit that there is this stubborn streak which runs through the breed. Some people say it is a sign of intelligence. Personally, I do not share that view but whatever the reason, stubbornness must not be allowed to succeed: the dog must do what he is commanded to do, not in his own time, when he feels like it, but immediately; and if it is done correctly, he should receive praise and lots of it. If it is not done, he is corrected and made to do it.

However, it is important that training sessions are properly and sensibly structured. A particular exercise should be repeated only a certain number of times during any one session, otherwise, the dog will become bored. If a dog enjoys his training sessions, they will be far more effective.

There are two golden rules in training. The first is: every command that is given must be obeyed. The second is: every command you give must be broken only by you, by which I mean do not tell your dog to sit then go off and make a cup of tea and forget all about him. You must release him from the command; if you allow him to break the command on his own, you are effectively untraining him.

Initial Training

It is a known fact that the treatment a puppy receives in the early stages of its life, even from weaning, will influence its whole future behaviour. The chances of achieving great things with your puppy increases if training begins at an early age. Obviously, rapport between you and your Rottweiler will be deeper if training is started while the dog is still quite young.

However, I have never started seriously training dogs at a very early age; I prefer to leave it until the puppy is about eight months old. But dogs can learn a lot by that age and may have picked up some very bad habits, so it is important that very basic training begins at eight weeks, and is increased in very gradual stages.

House Training

The first thing you will teach your Rottweiler puppy is to be clean in the house. It is important not to be brutal in this respect: one cannot expect a puppy to go all through the night and be clean in the morning – it is physically impossible. Paper should be left on the floor and the puppy encouraged to defaecate on it. The area of paper is decreased slightly each day and moved nearer the door. As the puppy gets older, he will want to go outside to the soiled piece of paper that you have positioned in a place that you may want him to use. Rubbing a dog's nose in his faeces is not effective and is not conducive to further training.

Lead Training

It is best if lead training is started quite young so that, as an older puppy, it will freely accept a check chain when it is placed around its neck. For a dog who has never had a collar, a check chain can be quite frightening. The collar should be introduced first to allow the puppy to become accustomed to wearing it. When the puppy has accepted it, the lead can be introduced.

When you take him out for his first walk on the lead, it is always nicer if an older dog accompanies you. The youngster will freely follow the older dog and soon become used to the collar and lead. No Rottweiler, no matter how good or bad, should be taken out without a lead on.

Car Training

Car training should be started as early as possible. Some puppies seem to be sick no matter what you do or how soon you accustom them to the car. It is best to start with a very short drive, just a mile or so and back home. For longer trips, there are travel sickness tablets especially for dogs and even those made for human consumption can be very beneficial if used according to the instructions for dosing a child. If your puppy is one of the few to suffer from travel sickness, it is best to get it started on tablets as soon as possible. The more the puppy is travel sick,

Ten-year-old Shelley Price with Anuschka v alt Mengenich SchH I ZTP. Over the frame.

the more it associates the car with a bad experience and the harder it is to break this association.

Recall

The initial stages of training a dog to recall start now. Every time you feed your puppy, call it by its name. When the puppy comes to you, put the food down. This is a simple recall which is immediately praised with the reward of dinner. It is very basic but very effective. In the same way, always try to make sure that when you are out with your puppy, you have a titbit in your pocket. When the puppy comes to your calling its name, reward it with a titbit, then put his lead on in your own time, praising and stroking it. Your puppy must be used to walking on the lead before you start any proper heel work training.

Joining a Club

If you are competing in general obedience, or in trials, the advantages of joining a club are many. Most Rottweiler clubs have training classes of their own although there are many all-breed dog training clubs that will accept Rottweilers. In these types of club, the trainers are trained rather than the dogs. Mistakes made by fellow members can be seen and eliminated from your own home training programme. It is no good going to a dog training club once a week and forgetting about it the rest of the week. That is not what the clubs are there for. You must train on your own for at least ten minutes a day. This is all that is required to have a really well-trained dog. If you want to progress to competition obedience, trials or Schutzhund, this is where you should start.

Some clubs are better than others, not all are interested in competition obedience, so if this is where your ambitions lie, make sure that the club you join is the type you are looking for. Many good books have been written about obedience; there are usually several to be found in any library. It is most beneficial for the novice trainer to read and fully understand one of these excellent books before he initiates his training programme.

Once you have mastered the initial stages of training, there are many great areas to progress to, including the mysteries of scent discrimination, one of the most fascinating aspects of the dog game and one which so many people, including show people who have been in the breed for many years, will never come to appreciaté.

Of all the obedience programmes designed to test dogs, I feel that the Schutzhund test is the most suited to the Rottweiler, although a close second must be the trials arena, which is built along very similar lines. The first stakes in this programme are CD (Companion Dog); the second stakes are UD (Utility Dog); the third, WD (Working Dog); the fourth TD (Tracking Dog) and the fifth PD (Police Dog). All these stakes are subdivided into other groups.

5

Kennelling and Diet

Whatever aspirations you have for your dog, a dog has basic needs. Most important is a warm, homely environment, where he is at peace with the world. This involves the company and love of his owners, pleasant walks, games and the correct diet. Also, a place to call his own, where he can retreat when he is tired. Leaving dogs for long periods of time, with no company; in a damp kennel, is a recipe for disaster, apart from being very cruel.

I feel sure that city life is not ideal for the Rottweiler. However, I am well aware that many Rottweilers do live happy, well-adjusted lives in towns although it is necessary to go to a great deal more trouble in order to ensure that some free running is made available. Again, extra care must be taken to ensure that you have permission of the landowner and, in these harrowing times, you must make sure no unsuspecting member of the public walks in on your game. A Rottweiler, at full speed, would flatten anyone in his path! To exercise a Rottweiler properly would, I suspect, necessitate a drive in the car for most city dwellers. Country dwellers do have a great advantage in this respect. We ourselves have well-fenced paddocks, where the dogs are turned out in couples, several times a day. Rabbiting and general sniffing about give way to sunbathing or swimming in our own natural pool.

It is important that a Rottweiler has time to develop his own character. Over the years, we have been asked to take back several dogs, for one reason or another, as most breeders do. I am always amazed at the change that occurs in their character.

Champion Blue Dale was taken back from a lady who used to show ponies. Owing to a riding accident, the lady was terrified of being knocked over by this lively young bitch and, consequently, shut her away for most of the day. When she came back to us, she was very shy and largely unhandled. You could say, almost wild. However, she has turned into a very special pet, who is the apple of her mistress's eye. Her finest achievement was to win the Best Bitch at Cruft's Dog Show. Her sister also came back to us, in more distressing circumstances. It took a lot longer to readjust this one but, again, it was worth it: she became Champion Jagen Blue Bhutia. Both bitches' characters improved in a friendly environment, so much so in fact that it is hard to get Dale to leave. She actually cries to come in to her 'Mum'.

Special care should be taken when considering kennelling. I feel that all dogs should have a kennel or somewhere to call their own. This applies as much to a one dog family, as it does to a larger set-up. It is not always possible to have a dog in the house and a kennel is ideal if it is designed properly: it must be warm but well ventilated, dry and well drained. This is his domain, where he can relax. All animals should have their own area or space.

Much of the evils of modern-day life can be attributed to overcrowding and lack of space. Tests on rats have proved that overcrowding produces aggression and antisocial behaviour. Consider the human child. Even he will make himself a special den, whether it be an old packing box, or under the stairs. He feels safe and protected. A dog will do the same thing. If no kennel is available, he will go behind the settee if it is against the wall and thus forming a small cave; or he will go behind the curtains if they fall to the floor – anywhere out of sight and covered on at least two sides. When you tell him off for a misdemeanour,

A home of his own!

this is where he will dive for shelter and wait until he thinks the coast is clear! This is a trait we have all observed and it is basic canine behaviour. Whether he is a small pup or a fully grown Rottweiler, the basic need of privacy is the same – somewhere to call his own.

Diet

The key to a proper diet is balance. A balanced diet contains all the essential nutrients in the correct amounts. This may seem hard work for the new Rottweiler owner, who may turn to an all-in-one type feed as a means of taking out the guessing element of feeding but it is important that food stuffs are both palatable and digestible. Some all-in-ones appear very good on paper, with impressive chemical analysis, but if they are not palatable, the dog's one highlight of the day – feed time – can be a great disappointment to him.

We also run a boarding kennel for all breeds, whose individual diets are so varied it is impossible to cater for every different one. However, over the years, we have found an all-in-one that does suit us and is liked by 90 per cent of our inmates. It comes in the shape of meal, which is

A diet should be palatable and digestible.

easily dampened with water, thus avoiding dehydration which is sometimes seen in dogs who are fed harder, very concentrated types of dry dog food. We do however mix in with it a small amount of tinned tripe, for no other reason than to make it more palatable and therefore more enjoyable for the dogs and, I can tell you, it makes all the difference – the food is eaten with great gusto.

Dogs need proteins, fats, water, vitamins and minerals and, to a lesser degree, carbohydrates. If you can find an all-in-one to suit you, fine; if not, your dog will probably be fed on a mixture of meat and biscuit.

Although the dog is a member of the mammalian Carnivora family, it is more truthful to describe him as an omnivore because he can live on a diet of animal derivatives or of vegetable origin. This is thought to be a direct result of his long ties with man.

If meat and biscuit are to be fed, it is important to ensure that all the elements of a balanced diet are included. Any elements that may be missing can be obtained from a wide range of vitamin and mineral supplements freely available on the pet market. It is strange how often one sees many cross-breeds looking in the peak of condition, having been fed table scraps, while some show animals appear to lack lustre, even though they are fed on the most expensively prepared pet foods available. I sometimes think the old adage of 'a little of what you fancy does you good' holds true, but basically, a dog must enjoy the food he is given, whether it is ready prepared all-in-one with a guaranteed nutritional value, or a home-made diet with added vitamins and minerals. For proper digestion, it must be palatable.

Sudden changes of diet should be avoided as sometimes, this can lead to diarrhoea. If a new foodstuff is to be introduced, it must be done slowly. When a dog is suffering from diarrhoea, the owner will often immediately blame the diet, which he immediately changes. Any dog with diarrhoea must have a complete fast day and if the condition does not clear up, consult your vet. A complete change in diet only makes things worse.

Most adult dogs are happy on one meal a day. However, the feeding requirements of one adult Rottweiler against another may be completely different. A dog's requirements largely depend on whether he is a working dog or non-working dog, old or young, sick or healthy, lives indoors or outdoors. This is where the prepared or complete dried foods are so useful: there is usually a feeding guide on the side of the bag, which takes all the guess-work out of feeding.

The kennel owner must keep a keen eye on all the dogs, to see if the feeding regime is totally suited to each particular dog and, if this is not so, a closer look must be taken to ascertain why. Some dogs are just bad doers, or have pancreas trouble and no amount of careful feeding can change their appearance.

Diet during Pregnancy and Lactation

Many bitches are overfed during pregnancy. An increase in food is made as soon as the bitch is mated. The fertilized eggs are not attached to the wall of the uterus until two to three weeks after mating and so extra food is not needed during this period. An increase can start four to five weeks after mating. In the last three weeks the foetuses will grow quickly; the bitch's requirements of energy and nutrients will increase and so 40 per cent extra food is needed during the last weeks of pregnancy. This 40 per cent increase should be reached in gradual stages, built up from the fourth week. The bitch will need to be fed several smaller meals, as opposed to her usual one a day.

Some bitches lose appetite just before whelping and, with our usually greedy bitches, it is a sure sign of the onset of whelping.

This bitch produced a record of seventeen puppies (ten of which were reared).

However, I have found some bitches not only eat immediately prior to whelping, but also devour all the afterbirth and look for another meal post-whelping. As this is usually deposited on the carpet afterwards, it should be avoided!

Loss of appetite that continues into lactation should receive veterinary advice immediately, as a good food supply is vital to produce the milk the pups are relying on. Lactation is probably the most demanding time nutritionally wise. A bitch's milk is very concentrated and requires a lot of food to produce. Between the second and fourth week, a Rottweiler bitch may need up to four times her normal daily intake, again delivered in small, easily digestible amounts, say four to five meals a day. As always, water should be unlimited, owing to the vast amount of milk being produced. We also give milk and sometimes a little honey for energy and generally spoil the bitch – they love it!

When the time comes to wean the pups, it should be done gradually. If pups are suddenly taken away, it will break the bitch's heart, or give her mastitis (see Chapter 8). The abrupt separation of puppies from mother is bad for all concerned, usually causing the puppies to go back several days.

We start our pups on canned tripe, with hot water poured over it. Allowed to cool, it forms a sort of soup. This is an excellent starter meal. Once this is being taken freely, you can start to add a finely broken down biscuit, all the time allowing the mum to return to clear up any left-overs.

You can start to wean pups at about two to three weeks of age. It must be remembered that the bitch's milk will remain a chief source of food supply to the pups until about four weeks, when gradual separation can begin. After complete separation, the bitch's food supply can be cut to slightly less than her ordinary maintenance diet. This will allow the milk to dry up. Once you have achieved dry-out, you must take a look at the bitch and decide what condition she is in. An increase in food may be in order, especially if she has reared a large litter. She may look run down, so, again, spoil her. She has done well.

Puppies

Puppies do little else other than eat, sleep and play. Your major job is keeping them clean: a large amount of food taken in must be passed out. When you consider that a puppy needs to eat large amounts of food in relation to its body weight, with only a small stomach capacity, it makes sense that meals must therefore be small and often.

If you think raising Rottweilers is easy, think again. If it is done properly, it is hard work. Four to five meals are the rule just after weaning. As the puppies grow, this can be reduced in gradual stages to four meals at about eight weeks old, when they leave for their new homes.

At this point, I must mention the fact that many breeders try to cram as much food down their puppies as possible, to try and increase growth and bone size. It has been proved on a test sample of pigs that over-feeding can be directly responsible for osteochondrosis and hip dysplasia. Supplements are also overdone: if the bottle or can says that you should give one spoonful, surely three would be even better? Quite the reverse: over-vitaminization causes breakdown of the bone structure.

So how should we feed our Rottweiler puppies? Many people have their own ideas and some simple rules apply. Our own feeding regime involves two milk feeds and two meat, usually with a bowl of hard, dry food left down to be fed ad lib. For the milk meal, we have had great success in the past with rice pudding, or a powdered milk especially designed for dogs mixed with some baby cereal to form a porridge. A meat meal usually consists of canned tripe. We used to use raw tripe, but after losing several puppies through problems caused by bacteria present in the raw tripe, we switched to the ready-cooked canned variety. This is mixed with very fine biscuit or meal with added supplements in the correct quantities. As I say, all breeders have their own ideas. It is a must to obtain a diet sheet when you collect your puppy. We give a diet sheet and enough food to last a week. The puppy is understandably under enough stress without changing its diet as well.

Puppies will be growing at a fast pace and so their nutritional needs are of great importance. Moderation is the key. Forced growth in Rottweilers can lead to many disorders and it is just not worth it. Pups fed properly will reach their genetic potential but at a more controlled rate. There are excellent foods on the market especially made for puppies. Take advice from other owners and breeders, or your vet. Remember, a happy puppy is not necessarily a fat puppy.

Essential Nutrients

Energy Food provides energy in the form of calories. A dog's energy needs are many: breathing, muscular activity, general body functions like maintaining the body heat all require energy. In short, energy is like fuel in a car. As we know, different quality fuels produce different results. Energy in food is produced from protein, fat and carbohydrate, which is oxidized or burned to release the energy. Fat produces twice the calories of carbohydrate, but overfeeding means the body has to store excessive calories in the form of body fat. Lack of food means poor growth and loss of condition.

Protein   There is an infinite variety of proteins. They provide the amino acids the body needs to grow and carry out repairs. Proteins have several important functions in the regulation of the metabolism, in the form of enzymes and hormones, which , as well as restructuring the body, also aid the transport of vital materials around the body. The dog's defence against diseases also totally relies on proteins. The quality of protein is very important, because the ability of the dog to absorb the available protein and not lose it in the faeces varies from one food stuff to another. In some foodstuffs, such as biscuit or cereal, as little as 50 per cent may be lost; in others, such as milk, up to 95 per cent may be lost. There are twenty amino acids to be found in protein, ten of which are essential. Milk and eggs provide the greatest amounts of essential amino acids. Protein deficiencies will result in poor growth or weight loss, dull coats and greatly reduced resistance to disease. 10 – 15 per cent protein is usually enough to form a maintenance diet, assuming the foodstuff is of good quality and easily digestible. Excess protein is stored as body fat.

Fat   Fat is a concentrated source of energy. Dogs crave fat in their diet. It makes most foods more palatable, although too much fat should be avoided. Up to 10 per cent is normal. Fats are broken down in the digestive system to form the fatty acids glycerin and glycerol and particularly linoletic acid. Any deficiency in linoletic acid causes re-productive disappointments. Dandruff and dry coats are another indication of this deficiency. This shortage is simple to top up, just by adding corn oil to the dog's diet. Incidentally, corn oil is a great help when the dog is changing his coat. The fatty acids also aid vitamin D (the sunshine vitamin) in the production of calcium.

Carbohydrate   A dog could live quite happily without any or with very little carbohydrate in his diet. For instance, we had a dog called Jagen Blue Andante, who from puppyhood would throw out any biscuit he found in his bowl. The mess this caused led us to feed him on a diet of raw tripe for the greater part of his life. He loved this diet and

112

grew to be a very handsome boy, winning the Top Puppy in the UK award.

Carbohydrate is not essential because dogs are able to synthesize their glucose needs from fat and protein. Dogs are, however, very good at converting carbohydrate as an energy source.

Carbohydrate comes in three forms: sugar, starches and indigestible polysaccharides (roughage). Dogs, like people, can form a sweet tooth and this should be discouraged. However, sugars are easy to digest and a good source of energy, but very fattening and bad for the teeth. Starches need to be cooked or broken down to be of any dietary value to the dog. Any cereal fed to a dog must be crushed. Even so, as you can see when you feed some ready prepared foodstuffs containing cereal, they may pass straight through in the faeces. Polysaccharides is a long name for roughage, or dietary fibre, which should not form more than 10 per cent of the dog's diet.

Vitamins Vitamins are needed to ensure normal health. Dogs are unable to synthesize them and so they must be restored on a daily basis. Only the fat-soluble vitamins A, D, E and K are stored. When fed in excess, A and D is retained in too great a quantity and will cause serious problems: an excess of vitamin A will cause bone malformation and an excess of vitamin D will cause calcification of the soft tissues.

Many of the calcium additives on the market contain Vitamin D, so it is of paramount importance not to exceed the directions on the product. Common sense must also come into play. I have heard of a person who brought several of the fashionable supplements and added the correct amounts from each product according to the manufacturer's instructions. Of course, each product overlapped the other in content, with the same vitamins being given several times. The end result was most disappointing.

If you are feeding a prepared all-in-one type food, the need for supplement should be negligible. Check the chemical analysis on the bag. Quality as ever varies. I am sorry to return to the same old theme but vitamins are needed in very small amounts, more is not better.

Mineral and Trace Elements Like vitamins, minerals are toxic if fed in excess. The likelihood of your dog having a mineral deficiency is extremely low, as most are commonly available in most foodstuffs. It is a misconception that Rottweilers, because of their greater size, must have little amounts of mineral supplements added to their foodstuffs, mainly calcium and phosphorous to aid bone construction. Judges who have in the past 'waxed lyrical' about the wonderful bone on certain dogs, even though their bone was probably man-made rather than genetic, have a lot to answer for! Rottweilers do not have bone in cart-horse proportions to their body size.

For every dog with exaggerated bone structure, several others face a life of lameness and pain from over-calciumization. No matter how much calcium you give a dog, there is a limit to the amount he can absorb. This is true until you increase vitamin D, when an increase in calcium absorption will be marked. If large amounts are then absorbed, damage to the edges of the bone occur, causing lameness, in one form or another. A classic case of 'never mind the quality, feel the width!'

Because of the greater volume of food eaten by a Rottweiler, the naturally occurring minerals should be quite sufficient to supply all their needs. Only in the case of growing youngsters or pregnant bitches would I advocate supplementation in very small amounts. Many a flyer as a puppy has broken down around the junior class stage. Forced puppies with their huge bones under stress from rapid growth will find joints becoming inflamed or even starting to break.

As with all feeding, a correct balance must be observed, but, in the case of minerals, the consequences of getting it wrong will be tragic. Owners who try to steal a march on their competitors will find themselves out of the game. Again, most prepared foods do it all for you; extra amounts of minerals will not be necessary.

Water   Water is an essential part of a dog's diet. It must be fresh and readily available at all times. It is necessary for daily functions, mainly to clear out waste products. To help in heat loss, water is lost through panting. A dog needs water for many other functions vital to life itself. A dog will die through water shortage far faster than he will through food shortage. Water must not be left down for days at a time or have insects floating in it. Water bowls must be frequently washed to avoid infection and build-up of algae.

Obesity

For some reason Rottweilers are one of the breeds most prone to suffer from obesity. Strangely, most owners do not even seem to know their pet is overweight. If it is pointed out to them, they usually reply 'Oh do you think so? I do not overfeed him, he just gets one meal a day'. They then go on to tell you that this meal is very small; the dog virtually lives on thin air! What they omit to tell you is that the dog probably scavenges most of his food - sweets from the children, next door's cat food from outside the back door, cream bun from Granny and so on! What these kind people do not realize is that they are killing the dog with kindness. The layer of excess body fat actually impairs the normal body functions. Another factor that contributes to obesity is lack of exercise. If a large dog does not receive sufficient exercise, he does not burn off the excess calories that can cause a weight problem. The reason most owners are not aware that their pet is overweight is that it is a gradual process, which develops over a period of time. Some of the consequences of obesity are very serious: arthritis, breathing difficulties, diabetes, heart failure, reproductive problems, skin disease, reduced resistance to disease and overheating caused by the thick jacket of fat under the skin.

Once you have recognized the problem, you must stop all feeding between meals. Make sure that everyone is aware of the problem and prepared to co-operate. Next consult your vet. There are some excellent obesity diets on the market. Some people cannot bring themselves to resist those appealing eyes that follow you everywhere; a hungry Rottweiler is an absolute pain. You are suddenly flavour of the month

Ch. Poirot Camilla, a picture of health. Owned by A.E. Wallett.

and the fat Rottweiler will wander after you from room to room with those big brown eyes. Don't give in.

One way to succeed in weight loss is to put your dog into boarding kennels when you go on holiday. Ask the kennel to put the dog on a strict diet for the weeks you are away. When you return, it is likely that enough weight will be lost for you to increase his exercise. Burn the rest off although it must be said that you should not over exercise fat Rottweilers. It puts intolerable strain on the heart and lungs. Take it steady at first. And buy him a few good quality bones, which tends to keep him happy while not providing much food value.

6

Schutzhund

The misconceptions about Schutzhund work are legion. People who are completely ignorant about Schutzhund training will decry the Schutzhund tests as a way of making Rottweilers more aggressive. Nothing could be further from the truth. Dogs who are taught to bite under command very rarely do so on their own initiative. To me, a trained dog will always be superior to an untrained, unreliable dog.

In discussing Schutzhund work, unknowledgeable people's focus is entirely on the man work section. However, there are three parts to a Schutzhund test. Part one is always tracking, which varies in length and time according to which stage you are at; Schutzhund I, II or III. The second section is always the obedience section, which involves heel work, retrieve, agility, reaction to gun shot and, most of all, control. The third section is protection work, with a very strong emphasis on protection, since the dog is being asked to protect his handler.

First of all, the Rottweiler is trained from a very early age to hold a small canvas sausage, which he is taught to hang on to and tug. As he gets older, the toy gets progressively bigger until he is presented with the canvas sleeve. I must point out that there is no animosity between the dog and the helper (or criminal). It is just a very advanced form of play and one which the dog dearly loves. It is simply a way of proving that the dog could perform a task if he were trained to do so, but this form of overarm sleeve is a complete safety catch. The dog will never attack anyone who does not have a sleeve on his arm. If a Schutzhund dog were sent forward towards the helper and the helper dropped the sleeve on the floor, the dog would take the sleeve and not the helper. I have explained this many times to many people and one of the reactions I get is 'What is the use of a dog that will only bite a sleeve?' The point is that it is a sport, purely a sport, and one which many German families regularly enjoy on Sunday afternoons.

In Germany, a check was made to find out if any of the biting incidents could be pinned on to dogs trained for the Schutzhund test. It was found that no dog who had been trained for Schutzhund work

A British dog is put through his paces by Kurt Schwenteck.

was involved in any biting incident in Germany for that year. To me this is a clear indication that Schutzhund dogs who are trained properly are more reliable and make better companions than untrained and un-educated dogs. However, it must be stressed that Schutzhund dogs should only be trained within the confines of a bona fide club. There is no room for amateurism in Schutzhund work.

I have a Schutzhund dog of my own and she is allowed to play quite happily with my children and other animals. In fact, in the home, she is one of our favourite dogs. The only time she becomes excited is when she sees the sleeve and I would say that is true for most Schutzhund dogs.

I must say I am very biased on this score because I love Schutzhund work. As a Championship Show judge who has trained a dog to Schutzhund qualification, I feel that I am qualified to comment. It is not really fair to associate the idiots who train their dogs to be aggressive with the highly trained Schutzhund dogs, who have taken years to reach perfection, spending long hard nights at the training club in the pouring rain and the snow, trekking over the fells or across the moors. Only someone who is really ignorant would mention these dogs in the same breath as the people who have disgraced our breed.

Schutzhund Examination I

Category A – Tracking (100 points)

Command: 'Seek'

The track is laid by the dog's own handler. It will be approximately 400 to 500 paces long, a minimum of twenty minutes old, with two articles for the dog to find. The dog must be handled on a 30-foot (10-metre) tracking leash.

The track must have two right (90-degree) angles which may be either to the right or to the left. The judge will determine the course of the track. The starting point will be marked.

After the handler has stood at the starting point for a short time, he must then walk the course as indicated by the judge and drop the first article at about the middle of the second leg without breaking stride. The second article must be placed at the end of the track and, after continuing a few paces in the same direction, the track-layer will return from the track.

Explanation: Before laying the track, the handler must show both articles to the judge. Only articles belonging to the handler may be used. They must be of neutral colour and not larger than a wallet. Search packages are not accepted. The handler's dog must be out of sight while the track is being laid. The track-layer must not scuff his feet or stop at any point. The articles must be laid directly on the track. The handler goes back to his dog to prepare him for tracking. Tracking can be performed with or without a tracking leash. When he is called upon, he will present himself with his dog to the judge, stating at this time whether his dog will pick up the articles or point them out. (A choice is given here, but the dog must perform as indicated, otherwise it will be considered a fault.)

When directed by the judge, the handler and his dog go quietly to the starting point and begin. Sufficient time is allowed for the dog to pick up the scent and no force is used at any time during the tracking. The dog should pick up the scent calmly, with a deep nose. As soon as the dog starts to track, the handler stands still and lets the 30-foot (10-metre) tracking leash pass through his hands. When the dog has reached the full extent of the leash, the handler will follow at this distance. As soon as the dog finds the first article, he should pick it up or point it out without any command from the handler. If the dog picks up the article, he can stand, sit or walk towards his handler. It is a fault for the dog to pick up the article and continue tracking. It is also a fault for the dog to lie down and then pick up the article although the dog trained to point out the article may stand, sit or lie down by the article. The handler drops his leash, goes to his dog, takes the article and holds it up to show that his dog has found it. Then the dog and the handler continue tracking. After completing the track, the handler must show both his articles to the judge.

Scoring: A faulty start, lack of control, circling on the track, constant encouragement from the handler, chewing or dropping of articles can result in deductions of up to four points. Repeat starting, lack of interest, tracking with a high nose, impetuous tracking, urinating or defaecating, can result in deduction of up to eight points. For missing an article ten points will be deducted. Overshooting the corners (angles) is not faulty, since wind conditions may carry the track's scent beyond the corner.

Category B – Obedience (100 points)

1. Heeling on Leash (15 points)   **Command:** 'Heel'
From the heeling position and on the command 'Heel', the dog should willingly heel beside his handler. The dog should always be on the left side of the handler, with his shoulder at the handler's knee.

On his own initiative, the handler must perform the prescribed heeling pattern conducted at normal, slow and fast paces. The normal and slow paces will include a left, right and about turn. Only when beginning from a stop or when changing the pace may a handler give the command 'Heel'. When the handler comes to a stop, the dog must sit automatically. The handler is not allowed to change his position to favour his dog. The handler must hold the leash loosely in his left hand. When indicated by the judge, the handler must heel his dog through a group of at least four moving people and he must stop at least once while doing this.

Explanation: At the beginning of the exercise, the dog and handler will go at least forty paces straight ahead without any stops or turns. A dog forging ahead, lagging behind, moving sideways, or the handler's helping the dog will be considered a fault.

2. Heeling off Leash (15 points)   **Command:** 'Heel'
While the dog and handler are heeling away from the group of four people, the judge will give the handler a signal to remove the leash. The

handler may put the leash in his pocket or place it over his shoulder. He must then return with his dog for the group heeling exercise. Dog and handler must then proceed through the group to perform at least one halt. After leaving the group, handler and dog must briefly come to a stop and continue with the exercise of heeling off the leash in the same pattern as heeling on leash. While handler and dog are performing this exercise, two pistol shots will be fired (not while walking through the group). The dog should not show any concern. If the dog shies away, he will be dismissed from the trial.

Explanation: If the dog becomes aggressive, but is still under the control of his handler, he will be faulted. Only the dog that shows stable behaviour will receive full points.

Note: Correct procedures must be followed when testing the dog for gun sureness. The shots must be fired at a distance of fifteen paces at an interval of ten seconds. If a dog runs away, he will be dismissed from the trial. If the judge is uncertain of whether or not the dog is truly gun-shy, he can repeat the test. The gun test will only be performed during heeling off leash and the long down under distraction.

3. Sitting Exercise (10 points) **Command:** 'Sit'
From the heeling position, the handler and his dog at heel and off leash must proceed straight ahead. After at least ten paces, the handler will tell his dog to sit and continues to walk without looking back or slowing down. The handler will go an additional thirty paces, stop, turn and face his dog. When directed by the judge, he will return to his dog and take up his position at the dog's right side. The dog must remain seated. If he stands up or lies down, he may lose up to five points as a result.

4. Down in Connection with Recall (10 points) **Commands:** 'Down', 'Come'
From the basic position, the handler must heel his dog off leash in a straight line. After ten paces and on the command 'Down', the dog must lie down immediately and the handler must continue to walk another thirty paces without looking back or changing pace. He must then turn around and when directed by the judge, call his dog. The dog must come quickly and willingly and sit directly in front of his handler. On the command 'Heel', the dog must move to the heeling position.

If the dog stands or sits, even if the recall is correct, up to five points may be deducted.

5. Retrieve Article belonging to Handler on Flat Ground (10 points)
Command: 'Fetch'
From a sitting position behind his handler, and on the command 'Fetch', the dog must retrieve off leash a personal article which has been thrown about ten paces away. The dog should retrieve quickly and, on his return, sit directly in front of his handler with the article in his mouth. After a pause, the handler must take the article on the command 'Give'. The dog must then return to the heeling position at the handler's side.

If the dog drops the article or plays with it, up to four points can be deducted. If the handler moves, three points will be deducted. If the dog does not retrieve, no points will be given. A dumb-bell may be used as a substitute for a personal article.

6. Retrieve over High Jump (1m/39in) (20 points) **Commands**: 'Over', 'Fetch'
The handler stands at a reasonable distance from the jump with his dog in the heeling position. The handler may throw either his own article or a dumb-bell over the hurdle. On the commands 'Over', 'Fetch,' the dog must jump the hurdle without touching it, retrieve, jump back over the hurdle and sit directly in front of his handler, holding the article in his mouth until the handler takes it on the command 'Give'. On the command 'Heel' the dog must assume the heeling position.

Scoring: Deductions will be made as follows:

Lightly touching the hurdle	2 points
Stepping on the hurdle	3 points
Hitting hurdle hard, dropping, playing or mouthing article	4 points
Return jump refused, article retrieved	10 points
Jump over refused, return jump correct, article retrieved	10 points
Going and coming jumps correct, article not retrieved	10 points
All jumps refused but article retrieved	All points
Going over completed, return jump refused, article not retrieved	All points

7. Go Ahead and Down (10 points)   **Commands**: 'Go', 'Down'
Off leash, in a direction indicated by the judge, the handler must walk with his dog in the heeling position. After a few paces, the handler should give his dog the command 'Go', raising his arm at the same time

as giving the vocal signal. The handler must stop, while his dog proceeds in the given direction at a fast pace. The dog must go a minimum of twenty-five paces before the handler gives the command 'Down'. The dog must lie down immediately. The handler may keep his arm raised until the 'Down' command is given. When directed by the judge, the handler will walk to his dog's right side to assume a heeling position and give the command 'Sit'.

Repetitious arm signals are not allowed. The dog must go in a straight line as indicated. Points will be deducted for a large deviation in direction, slowness in going down, going down before a command, or getting up before the exercise is completed.

8. Long down under Distraction (10 points)

At the start of the first dog's obedience exercises, the handler of the second dog will be instructed to put his dog on a down about forty paces away. The dog must be off leash and there must be no article of any kind left with him. In sight of the dog, the handler walks away without looking back and stands about forty paces away with his back to the dog. The dog must remain down while the other dog performs exercises 1 to 6. The handler will stand quietly until instructed by the judge to pick up his dog. The handler will walk to his dog's side and give the command 'Sit'.

For any help the handler may give his dog or for the dog getting up before the handler returns, points will be deducted. Partial credit can only be given if the dog remains down from exercise 1 to 3.

Category C – Protection (100 points)

1. Hold at Bay and Bark (5 points)　　Command: 'Search'

The helper is placed in hiding, about forty paces away, to give the dog a chance to search at least once to the right or left. While the helper takes up his hiding place, the handler and the dog must be out of sight. When instructed by the judge, the handler must send his dog to search with the command 'Search' or 'Find'. Upon finding the helper, the dog should not bite, but stay close to him and bark, holding him at bay. The handler remains about twenty-five paces away until advised to go and pick up his dog. The handler and his dog must then leave the field and remain out of sight.

2. Attack on the Handler (30 points)

Now the helper takes a new hiding place about fifty paces away from the starting point. When instructed by the judge, the handler must heel his dog on a leash, in a given direction. After about twenty-five paces, the handler will unleash his dog and put the leash away. Without breaking stride, he must continue to walk with his dog at heel. Suddenly, the helper will leave his hiding place and attack the handler from the front. Contact between handler and helper is not allowed. The dog must immediately attack the helper and bite hard. At this point the helper will hit the dog twice with a switch $^3/_8$in (1cm) in diameter on the less sensitive parts of the dog's body. The handler may only encourage his dog vocally. On a signal from the judge, the helper must stand still. Slight encouragement for the dog's benefit is permissible at this point. The dog will be given the command 'Leave' and he must release his bite.

3. Pursuit and Hold at Bay (Courage Test) (55 points)
When the dog has released his bite in the previous exercise, the handler must hold him by the collar. The helper will then run in a straight line away, making threatening gestures. When the helper has gone about fifty paces, the handler must send his dog after him and remain at the spot from where the dog was sent. The judge will signal when the dog is about thirty paces from the helper. The helper will then run towards the dog, using exaggerated threatening gestures. When contact is made, the helper should not use the switch. If the dog holds onto the helper, the attack should stop. If the dog refuses to let go after the 'Leave' command, the handler will wait until directed by the judge to take his dog off. After the dog releases the helper, the handler should wait approximately thirty seconds without influencing his dog in any way. Then when directed by the judge, the handler must approach the helper and conduct a search. He must then put his dog on a leash, stepping to the right side of the helper and transporting him to the judge.

Explanation: While approaching the helper's hiding place, the dog must remain at heel on the left side of the handler. The dog will lose up to three points by moving forward and leaving his handler's side. After the attack, the helper does not have to stand still, but rather turn with the dog to protect himself, without being aggressive. Only the hard-biting dog who also lets go on a single command can and will receive full points.

The command 'Leave' is, in all phases, allowed only once. Dogs who bite again after the command 'Leave' is given, or those who will not let go properly, can be penalized up to fifteen points. Dogs who do not let go in all phases cannot receive the Schutzhund Degree.

Commands other than 'Leave' are not allowed. If the dog avoids the switch, he must renew the attack on his own. If the dog returns to the handler, or does not remain by the helper to watch him, only partial points can be awarded for 'Courage And Hardness'. Only dogs who show exceptional courage will receive full points.

Note: Any dog, even though he may have passed the temperament test before the trial, can be dismissed by the judge during the trial if the dog shows obvious signs of unsoundness.

Schutzhund Examination II

Category A – Tracking (100 points):

Command: 'Find It'

The track will be laid by a stranger. It must be approximately 600 to 700 paces long and at least thirty minutes old. Two articles and a 30-foot (10-metre) tracking leash are to be used. The track must have two right (90-degree) angles, either to the right or to the left. The starting point will be marked. After the track-layer has stood at the starting point for a short time, he will proceed to walk the course as indicated by the judge. He will drop the first article without breaking his stride, at about the middle of the second leg. The second article will be laid at the end of the track and after a few paces the track-layer will return from the track.

Explanation: Before laying the track, the track-layer has to show both articles to the judge. Only articles with the scent of the track-layer will be used. They should be of neutral colour and not larger than a wallet. So called search packages are not acceptable. During the laying of the track the handler and his dog will be out of sight. The odour of the track should not be changed by the track-layer by standing still or scraping his feet across the ground. The articles should be laid directly on the track, not beside it.

The handler will now get his dog ready for tracking. When called upon, he must present himself and his dog to the judge, stating at this time whether his dog will pick up the articles or point them out. When directed by the judge, the handler must take his dog slowly and calmly to the start of the track. The handler should give his dog sufficient time to pick up the scent and the dog should pick up the scent calmly with a deep nose.

As soon as the dog starts tracking, the handler will let the 30-foot (10-metre) leash pass through his hands to its fullest extent before following the dog at the end of the leash. When the dog reaches the first article, he should, without command from the handler, either pick it up or point it out (as indicated to the judge beforehand). After picking up the article, the dog may either stand-stay, sit-stay or return to the handler. Any continuing on the track after picking up the article is a fault. The pointing out may be done by standing, sitting or downing. The handler must drop the leash and walk up to his dog immediately. By holding the article over his head, the handler must show to the judge that the dog has found the article. Following this, the handler and his dog must continue on the track. When finished with the track, the handler must show both articles to the judge.

Scoring: A faulty start, lack of control, circling on the track, constant encouragement from the handler, chewing or dropping of articles may result in deductions of up to four points. Repeat starting, lack of interest, tracking with a high nose, impetuous tracking, urinating or defaecating, may result in deductions of up to eight points. For a wrongly picked up or pointed our article, four points will be deducted. For missing an article, ten points will be deducted. Overshooting the corners is not faulty, since the wind may carry the track's scent beyond the corner.

Note: At no time should a handler resort to force while tracking his dog.

Category B – Obedience (100 points)

1.   Heeling on Leash (10 points)   **Command**: 'Heel'
From the heeling position, the dog should heel willingly on a loose leash. The dog should always position himself with his shoulder beside the left knee of the handler and he should not forge ahead, follow behind, or stay off to the side. On his own initiative, the handler must perform the prescribed heeling pattern at normal, slow and fast paces. The normal and slow paces will include a left, right and about turn. Turn-abouts must be performed to the left only. Only at the start and when changing the pace is the handler allowed to give the dog the command 'Heel'. When the handler comes to a stop, the dog should sit automatically without an additional command. The handler may not

change his position to favour his dog. During this exercise the leash should be loosely held in the left hand. When directed by the judge, the handler must heel his dog through a group of at least four moving people. The handler must come to a halt at least twice while heeling through the group. At the start of the exercise, it is required that the handler and his dog proceed for at least fifty paces in a straight line without any turns or halts.

2.   Heeling off Leash (15 points)   **Command**: 'Heel'
While the dog and the handler are heeling away from the group in exercise 1, the judge will give the handler a signal to remove the leash. The handler may place the leash around his shoulder or in his pocket. Dog and handler must then proceed through the group, to perform at least one halt. After leaving the group, the handler and dog must stop briefly before continuing with the exercise of heeling off leash in the same pattern as 'Heeling on Leash'. While the handler and his dog are going through the heeling exercise (but not while moving through the group) two shots will be fired. The dog should behave impartially to the gunshots. If the dog proves gun-shy, he will be disqualified from the examination.

Explanation: Should the dog show aggressiveness, but remain under control of the handler, this will only be considered a fault. Full points can only be given to the dog that is impartial to gun shots.

Note: Correct procedure must be followed when testing for gun sureness. The gunshots should be fired at a distance of fifteen paces at an interval of ten seconds. If a dog should run away after a gunshot, he will be disqualified from the examination. If a judge suspects that a dog is gun-shy, he may choose to test the dog further. The testing for gun-shyness will only be done under the exercise, 'Heeling off Leash', and 'Long down under Distraction'.

3.   Sitting Exercise (while moving) (5 points)   **Command**: 'Sit'
Out of the heeling position, the handler must heel his dog off leash and proceed straight ahead. After a minimum of ten paces, he must give his dog the command 'Sit'. The dog should sit immediately without the handler changing his pace. After another thirty paces, the handler must stop, turn around and face his dog. When directed by the judge, the handler must return to his dog. If the dog, instead of sitting, lies down or stands, he will lose up to three points.

4. Down in connection with Recall (10 points)   **Commands**: 'Down', 'Come'

The handler must heel his dog off leash in a straight line and after at least ten paces, down his dog. The dog should go down immediately and the handler must continue to walk another thirty paces without looking back or changing his pace. He must then turn around and, when directed by the judge, call his dog. The dog should come at a fast pace and sit directly in front of his handler. When given the command 'Heel', the dog should then assume the heeling position. If the dog should sit or stand, even if the recall is correct, he will lose up to five points.

5. Retrieve of a 2lb (1kg) Dumb-Bell on Flat Ground (10 points)
Command: 'Fetch'

The handler must stand with his dog at heel and throw the dumb-bell approximately ten paces. After the command 'Fetch', the dog should immediately run and pick up the dumb-bell, bringing it back to the handler. The dog should then sit directly in front of the handler with the dumb-bell in his mouth. After a brief pause, the handler should then give the dog the command 'Give' and take the dumb-bell. When given the command 'Heel', the dog should go to the left side of the handler and assume the heeling position.

Scoring: If the dog drops the dumb-bell, plays with it or chews it, he will lose up to four points. If the dog handler changes his position during the exercise, he will lose up to three points. If the dog does not retrieve, he cannot receive any points for this exercise.

6. Retrieve of a 1½ lb (0.75kg) Dumb-Bell over a 39in (1m) High Jump (15 points)   **Commands**: 'Over', 'Fetch'

The handler stands with his dog at a reasonable distance from the jump. He must then throw the dumb-bell over the jump. When given the command, the dog should go over the jump without touching it, pick up the dumb-bell, return over the jump and sit in front of his handler. When given the command 'Give', the dog should release his hold and the handler take the dumb-bell.

Scoring: For lightly touching the jump, two points may be deducted. For lightly stepping on the jump, up to three points. For hitting the jump hard, dropping the article, playing or chewing, up to four points may be deducted. Points will be awarded as follows:

Jump and retrieve correct	15 points
First jump correct, return jump refused, retrieve correct	8 points
First jump refused, return jump correct, retrieve correct	8 points
Both jumps correct, retrieve refused	8 points
Both jumps and retrieve refused	No points
First jump correct, return jump, retrieve refused	No points

If the dumb-bell should land beside the jump, the handler may with the judge's permission, retrieve the dumb-bell and throw it again. No automatic point deduction should be made. If the dog drops the article, the judge may repeat the exercise to determine if the dog is just confused or unwilling to work. The handler should remain in his original position until the exercise is completed.

7. Retrieval over a 6ft (2m) Climbing Wall of an Article (or Dumb-Bell) Belonging to the Handler (15 points)   Command: 'Over' 'Fetch'

Handler and dog stand at a reasonable distance from the jump. On command, the dog should scale the wall, pick up the article, return over the wall and sit directly in front of the handler. He should hold the article until given the command 'Give'. The handler must take the article. On the command 'Heel' the dog must assume the heeling position.

Explanation: The command 'Fetch' must be given before the dog picks up the dumb-bell.

Scoring: For dropping, playing or chewing the article, up to four points can be deducted.

Jump and retrieve correct	15 points
First jump correct, return jump refused, article retrieved	8 points
First jump refused, return jump and retrieve correct	8 points
First and return jump correct, retrieve refused	8 points
First, return jump and retrieve refused	No points
First jump correct, return jump and retrieve refused	No points

If the article or dumb-bell should land beside the jump, the handler may, with the judge's permission, retrieve the article and throw it again. No automatic point deduction should be made. If the dog drops the article, the judge may repeat the exercise to determine if the dog is just confused or unwilling to work. The handler should remain in his original position until completion of the exercise.

8. Go Ahead and Down (10 points)   **Commands**: 'Go', 'Down'

Off leash in a direction indicated by the judge, the handler will walk with his dog at heel. After a few paces, the handler should give his dog the command 'Go' by raising his arm at the same time as the vocal command. The handler should stop while his dog proceeds in the given direction at a fast pace. The dog must go a minimum of thirty paces and then go down immediately on one command. The handler may keep his arm raised pointing out the direction to his dog until the 'Down' command is given. When directed by the judge, the handler must walk to his dog. When the dog is picked up by the handler, the command 'Sit' must be given.

Explanation: Repeated arm and vocal commands are to be considered faulty. The dog should go out in a straight line, but a slight drifting is not faulty. Changing direction, not going out far enough, lying down too soon or standing before the handler picks him up will result in a deduction of points.

9. Down under Distraction (10 points)   **Command**: 'Down'

At the start of the first dog's obedience exercise the handler of the second dog will be instructed to put his dog on a down about forty paces away. The dog should be off leash and there must be no article of any kind left with him. In sight of the dog, the handler must stand forty paces away with his back to the dog. The dog should stay down without any influence from the handler until the first dog completes the exercises 1 to 7. After exercise 7, the handler will be instructed to pick up his dog.

Explanation: The handler must stand quietly in his original position until advised by the judge to pick up his dog. For any help the handler may give his dog, or for the dog getting up too early, points will be deducted. No points can be given unless the dog remains down during exercises 1 to 5.

Category C – Protection (100 points)

1. Searching for the Agitator (5 points)   **Command**: 'Search'

The helper is placed in hiding to allow the dog a search to the left and right five to six times. While the helper goes into hiding, the dog and handler must be out of sight. When the handler raises his arm and gives the dog the command, the dog should leave the handler and search to

Atze v Eylauer-Høf, SchH III, with handler during 'Search of Criminal'.

the right and to the left. The handler is allowed to assist his dog as often as necessary and may call his dog back to heel before sending him in another direction. Should the dog search occasionally to the rear, it is not considered a fault. The handler should stay in the imaginary centre line of the search area.

2.   Finding and Barking (10 points (5+5))
As soon as the dog finds the helper, the handler should stand still while his dog barks continuously at the helper. When instructed by the judge, the handler must walk within four paces of the hiding place and down his dog approximately three to four paces away. He should search the helper and then his hiding place for anything he may have left there.

Scoring: For continuously barking, the dog will receive five points. If the dog only barks lightly, two points may be deducted. If he does not bark at all, five points will be deducted. If the non-barking dog stays with the helper without biting, he will receive five of the ten points. For lightly biting the helper, he will lose up to two points. For hard biting, he will lose up to four points.

131

3.   Escape and Defence (Escape – 10 points, Defence – 30 points)
The judge will now instruct the helper to run away from the dog and try to escape. The dog should prevent this by biting hard. The helper should end his escape attempt by standing still and the dog should now release his hold. When instructed by the judge, the helper should attack the dog, threatening him with a switch without actually hitting him. The dog should attack immediately and, by biting hard, stop the helper from fighting. After the dog obtains a firm hold, he should be hit twice with the switch on the less sensitive parts of his body. Only after being instructed by the judge should the handler go to the helper to search for weapons. The handler should not take the switch away from the helper, but it should be carried so that the dog does not see it until exercise 5. Before the search is conducted, he should put his dog in a down or sit to watch the helper.

Explanation: The helper should wear a coat, jacket or sleeve as protection. As soon as the dog takes a firm hold, it is absolutely necessary that he strike the dog twice with a switch. At no time should the dog try to avoid the blows.

4.   Transport (5 points)
Now follows the transport of the helper for about forty paces. The handler calls his dog to heel and then instructs the helper to walk ahead while he and his dog follow about five paces behind.

5.   Attack, Courage Test, Fighting Instinct (40 points)
a) Attack and Courage Test (30 points).
During the transport, the helper will attack the handler. After a firm bite, the attack should stop and the handler should call his dog off, holding him by the collar. The helper will walk away and, after approximately fifty paces make a threatening motion before running away. The handler must now release his dog to send him after the helper. When the dog is about half way between the helper and the handler, the judge will instruct the helper to turn around. While making threatening gestures with the switch, he will run towards the dog, but not to strike him at this time. The dog must bite hard immediately, while the handler remains at a distance of thirty paces. When commanded by the handler, the dog should release his hold. The handler must now stand motionless for about thirty seconds without influencing the dog. If the dog, when commanded to release, does not let go, the handler, upon further instruction, should go immediately to

take his dog off. Now follows the side transport of the helper back to the judge, who is about forty paces away. After completing this phase, the handler will leave the field with his dog on leash.

b) Fighting Instinct including Courage and Hardness (10 points).
The judge will have to observe the fighting instinct of the dog during all the exercises in order to evaluate him accurately. The dog forging towards the helper and hard biting are some signs of the dog's fighting instinct. Should the dog avoid blows, he should immediately renew the attack on his own. Should the dog return to the handler during the courage test or stay close to the helper without watching him (sniffing, running around and so on), he can only receive partial credit. Full points for fighting instinct can only be given to dogs who demonstrate exceptional courage and hardness.

Explanation: The command 'Leave' is, in all phases, allowed only once. Dogs who bite again after the command 'Leave' is given or those who will not let go properly, can be penalized by up to fifteen points. Dogs who do not let go in all phases cannot receive the Schutzhund Degree.
     Whenever the dog releases his hold, the helper does not have to stand completely motionless if it is necessary to move in order to see the dog. However, in no circumstances should he make threatening motions. He should always protect himself and only stand completely motionless if the dog stands waiting in front of him. Only the energetic attacking and hard-biting dog, who releases immediately after one command, can receive all the points.
     No commands other than 'Leave' are permissible.

Note: If the dog has passed the temperament test prior to the examination, but later shows obvious signs of unsoundness, he may then be excused from the examination.

Schutzhund Examination III

Category A – Tracking (100 points)

Command: 'Seek'.
The track will be laid by a stranger. It will be approximately 1,200 to 1,400 paces long and at least fifty minutes old using three articles. The

track includes at least four right angles and the starting point should be marked. After the track-layer has stood at the starting point for a short time, he will then proceed to walk the course as indicated by the judge without breaking his stride. He will drop the first article after about a hundred paces, the second article half-way into the second or third leg and the third will be dropped at the end of the track. After dropping the last article, he will then proceed for a few more paces and then walk away from the track. The dog may track either freely or on a 30-foot (10-metre) leash. Both ways will be judged identically.

Explanation: Before laying the track, the track-layer has to show the articles to the judge. Only articles with the scent of the track-layer can be used. They should be of neutral colour and not larger than a wallet. So-called search packages are not acceptable. During the laying of the track, the handler and his dog will be out of sight. The odour of the track should not be changed by the track-layer by standing still or scraping his feet across the ground. The articles should be laid directly on the track and not beside it. The handler will now get his dog ready for tracking. When called upon, the handler must present himself and his dog to the judge, stating at the time whether his dog will pick up the articles or point them out.

When directed by the judge, the handler must take his dog slowly and calmly to the start of the track. No force should be used at any time while tracking. The handler should give his dog sufficient time to pick up the scent. The dog should pick up the scent calmly with a deep nose. As soon as the dog starts tracking, the handler will let the 30-foot (10-metre) leash pass through his hands and follow the dog at the end of the leash. When the dog reaches the first article, he should without command either pick it up or point it out (as indicated to the judge beforehand).

After picking up the article, the dog may either stand-by, sit-stay or he may return to the handler. Any continuing on the track after picking up the article is a fault. The pointing out may be done by standing, sitting or downing. The handler must drop the leash and walk up to his dog immediately. By holding the article over his head, the handler should show the judge that the dog has found the article. Following this, the handler and his dog continue on the track. When the track is completed, the handler must show all three articles to the judge.

Scoring: A faulty start, lack of control, circling on the track, constant encouragement or chewing or dropping of the articles will result in a

134

deduction of up to four points. Repeat starting, lack of interest, tracking with a high nose, impetuous tracking and urinating or defaecating result in deductions of up to eight points. For a wrongly picked up or pointed out article, four points will be deducted. For missing an article, seven points will be deducted. Overshooting the corners is not faulty since wind conditions affect the track's scent and may carry it beyond the corner.

Category B – Obedience (100 points)

1. Heeling off Leash (10 points) **Command**: 'Heel'
The handler should report to the judge with his dog off leash. The handler will carry the leash keeping it out of sight of the dog. The dog should heel willingly and happily with his shoulder beside the left knee of the handler and he should not forge ahead, follow behind or stray off to the side. On his own initiative, the handler must perform the heeling pattern at normal, fast and slow paces. The normal and slow paces should include a left, right and about turn. Only at the start and when changing the pace is the handler allowed to give the dog the command 'Heel'. When the handler comes to a stop, the dog should sit automatically without an additional command. The dog handler may not change his position to favour his dog. When directed by the judge, the handler must heel his dog through a group of at least four moving people. The handler has to come to a halt at least twice while heeling through the group. At the start of the exercise, the handler and his dog should proceed for at least fifty paces in a straight line and return with-out a halt. Turn-abouts must be performed to the left only. While the handler and his dog are going through the heeling exercises (but not while moving through the group) two gunshots will be fired. The dog should behave impartially to the gunshots. If the dog is gun-shy, he will be excused from the examination. Should the dog show aggressiveness, but remain under control of the handler, it will only be considered a fault. Full points can only be given to the dog that is impartial to gunshots.

Note: Correct procedure must be followed when testing the dog for gun-sureness. The shots should be fired at a distance of fifteen paces, at an interval of ten seconds. If a dog runs away after a gunshot, he will be excused from the examination. If the judge feels that a dog is gun-shy, he may choose to further test the dog. The testing for gun-shyness will only be done under the exercise 'Heeling off Leash' and 'Long down under Distraction'.

2.   Sitting Exercise (while moving) (5 points)   **Command**: 'Sit'
Out of the heeling position, the handler and his dog will heel off leash straight ahead. After a minimum of ten paces he will give his dog the command 'Sit'. The dog should sit immediately, without the handler changing pace. After another thirty paces, the handler should turn around facing the dog. When directed by the judge, the handler should turn around facing the dog. When directed by the judge, the handler should return to his dog. If the dog, instead of sitting, lies down or stands, he will lose up to three points.

3.   Down in Connection with Recall (10 points)   **Commands**: 'Down', 'Come'
Out of the basic position, the handler will heel his dog in a straight line for at least ten paces. At this point, the handler will begin to run. After another ten paces, he must down his dog without interrupting his pace and continue to run to a designated hiding place. After approximately one minute, when directed by the judge, he must appear out of the hiding place and, upon further instruction, call his dog. The dog should come immediately at a fast pace and sit directly in front of the handler. On the command 'Heel', the dog should assume the heeling position.

Explanation: If the dog sits or stands, he will lose up to five points.

4.   Standing Exercise (while moving) (5 points)   **Command**: 'Stand'
From a heeling position, the handler will heel his dog off leash in a straight line. After about ten paces, when told to 'Stand', the dog should stand-stay immediately. Without turning around or changing his pace, the handler should walk another thirty paces, turn around and face his dog. When directed by the judge, he must return to his dog. The exercise is completed after the handler has returned to the dog, ordered him to sit and the dog has actually come to a sit position.

5.   Standing Exercise (while running) (10 points) **Commands**: 'Stand', 'Come'
On completion of exercise 4, the handler must immediately heel his dog while running for at least ten paces. He must then tell his dog to 'Stand' and, without interrupting his pace, continue for another thirty paces. He must then turn around to face his dog and, when directed by the judge, call his dog. The dog should come immediately at a fast pace and sit directly in front of his handler. When given the command 'Heel', the dog should assume the heeling position.

Explanation: If the dog sits or lies down after being given the command 'Stand', he will lose up to five points. Any movement of the dog after the command 'Stand' is considered faulty.

6. Retrieve of a 4lb (2kg) Dumb-Bell on Flat Ground (10 points)
Command: 'Fetch'

The handler must stand with his dog at heel and throw the dumb-bell approximately ten paces. On the command 'Fetch', the dog should immediately run to pick up the dumb-bell and bring it back to the handler. The dog should sit directly in front of the handler with the dumb-bell in his mouth. After a brief pause, the handler should give the command 'Out' and take the dumb-bell. When given the command 'Heel', the dog should go to the left side of the handler and assume a heeling position.

Explanation: If the dog drops the dumb-bell, plays with it or chews it, he may lose up to four points. If the dog handler changes his position during the exercise, he may lose up to three points. If the dog does not retrieve, he cannot receive any points for this exercise.

7. Retrieve of a 1½lb (0.75kg) Dumb-Bell over a 39in (1m) High Jump (15 points)   **Commands**: 'Over', 'Fetch'

The handler stands with his dog at a reasonable distance from the jump. He must then throw the dumb-bell over the jump. When given the command, the dog should go over the jump without touching it, pick up the dumb-bell and return over the jump to sit in front of his handler. When given the command 'Out', the dog should release his hold and the handler take the dumb-bell.

Explanation: The command 'Fetch' must be given before the dog picks up the dumb-bell.

Scoring: For lightly touching the jump two points may be deducted. For lightly stepping on the jump, up to three points may be deducted. For hitting the jump hard, dropping the article, or playing or chewing, up to four points may be deducted. Points shall be awarded as follows:

Jump and Retrieve correct	15 points
First jump correct, return jump refused, retrieve correct	8 points
First jump refused, return jump and retrieve correct	8 points

Both jumps correct, refusal to retrieve   8 points
Both jumps and retrieve refused   No points
First jump correct, return jump and retrieve refused   No points

If the dumb-bell lands beside the jump, the handler may, after asking the judge, pick up the dumb-bell and throw it again. No automatic point deduction should be made. If the dog drops the article, the judge may repeat the exercise to determine if the dog is just confused or unwilling to work. The handler should remain in his original position until the exercise is completed.

8.   Retrieve over a 6ft (2m) Climbing Wall of an Article (or Dumb-Bell) Belonging to the Handler (15 points)   Commands: 'Over', 'Fetch'

The handler and his dog should stand at a reasonable distance from the wall. When given the command, the dog should scale the wall, pick up the article (or dumb-bell), return over the wall and sit directly in front of the handler. He should hold the article until the handler gives the command 'Out'. On releasing the article, the dog will be given the command 'Heel'.

Scoring: For dropping the article, playing or chewing, up to four points can be deducted. Points shall be awarded as follows:

Jump and Retrieve correct   15 points
First jump correct, return jump refused, article retrieved   8 points
First jump refused, return jump correct, retrieve correct   8 points
First and return jumps correct, retrieve refused   8 points
First, return jump and retrieve refused   No points
First jump correct, return jump and retrieve refused   No points

If the article or dumb-bell lands beside the jump, the handler may, with the permission of the judge, retrieve the dumb-bell and throw it again. No automatic deductions should be made. If the dog drops the article, the judge may repeat the exercise to determine if the dog is just confused or unwilling to work. The handler should remain in his original position until completion of the exercise.

9.   Go-ahead and Down (10 points)   Commands: 'Go', 'Down'

Off leash, in a direction indicated by the judge, the handler must walk with his dog in a heeling position. After a few paces, the handler should raise his arm and give the command 'Go'. As the handler comes to a halt, the dog should proceed at a fast pace for at least another forty paces in the direction indicated. When given the command 'Down', he should go down immediately. The handler may keep his arm raised, pointing out the direction to his dog until the 'Down' command is given. When directed by the judge, the handler must then walk to his dog and give the command 'Sit'. This finishes the exercise.

Explanation: Repeated arm and vocal commands are considered faulty. The dog should go in a straight line, but a slight drifting is not faulty. Changing direction, not going out far enough, lying down too soon or standing up before the handler picks him up may result in point deductions.

10.   Down under Distraction (10 points)   **Command**: 'Down'
At the beginning of the first dog's obedience exercises, the handler of the second dog must down his dog and leave him. The handler must then go to a designated hiding place at least forty paces away. The handler must remain out of sight until called by the judge. The dog must remain down throughout exercises 5 to receive any points.

Category C – Protection (100 points)

1.   Searching for the Helper (5 points)   **Command**: 'Search'
The helper is placed in hiding to allow the dog to search to the left and right five to six times. While the helper goes into hiding, the dog and handler have to be out of sight. When the handler raises his arm and gives the command, the dog should leave the handler and search to the right and to the left. The handler is allowed to help his dog as often as necessary and may call his dog back to heel before sending him in another direction. Should the dog search occasionally to the rear, it is not considered a fault. The handler should stay in the imaginary centre line of the search area.

2.   Finding and Barking (10 points (5+5))
As soon as the dog finds the helper, the handler should stand still and the dog should bark continuously at the helper. When instructed by the judge, the handler should walk within four paces of the hiding place and upon further instruction call his dog to heel. The handler must then ask the helper to leave his hiding place. The handler must down his dog approximately three to four paces away. He should search the helper and then his hiding place for anything he may have left there.

Scoring: For continuous barking, the dog will receive five points. If the dog only barks lightly, two points may be deducted. If the dog does not bark at all, five points will be deducted. If the non-barking dog stays with the helper without biting, he will receive five of the ten available points. For lightly biting the helper he will lose two points. For hard biting, he will lose up to four points.

3.   Escape and Defence (Escape – 10 points, Defence – 20 points)
The judge will instruct the helper to run away and try to escape. The dog should prevent this by biting hard. The helper should stop his attempt to escape by standing still and the dog should now release his hold. When instructed by the judge, the helper should now attack the dog, threatening the dog with a switch without actually striking him. The dog should attack immediately and by biting hard, should stop the helper from fighting. After the dog obtains a firm hold, he should be hit twice with a switch on the less sensitive parts of his body. Only after being instructed by the judge should the handler go to the helper to search for weapons. The handler should not take the switch away from the helper, but it should be carried so that the dog does not see it until exercise 5. Before the handler searches the helper, he should down his dog to watch the helper.

Explanation: The helper should wear a coat, jacket or sleeve as protection. As soon as the dog takes firm hold, it is absolutely necessary that he strike the dog twice with a switch. At no time should the dog try to avoid the blows.

4.   Transport (5 points)
Now follows the back transport of the helper for about fifty paces. The handler must call his dog to heel and then instruct the helper to walk ahead while he and his dog follow approximately five steps behind.

5.   Attack and Test of Courage (40 points (10+10+20))
  a)   During the transport the helper will attack the handler. The dog should respond to this assault by taking a firm bite. After the attack, a search should be made and the helper disarmed. Now follows a side transport to the judge. After this is completed, the handler must leave with his dog at heel and go into hiding.
  b)   At a distance of about a hundred paces, the judge will direct the helper into a hiding place. The dog handler will be instructed to take a position from which his dog must overcome and stop

140

the escapee. When instructed by the judge, the helper will leave his hiding place and after being challenged by the handler, will run away. The handler must now send his dog out to stop the helper. The dog should use the shortest distance to catch the helper. When the dog gets to within about forty paces, the helper will turn around and try to chase the dog away. Without being deterred, the dog should bite hard and hold the helper. The handler may approach up to a distance of forty paces after sending his dog out. The helper will now stand still, after which the dog should release his hold.

c) The helper will once more proceed to attack the dog, at which point he will use the switch to frighten him. After the dog has obtained a firm hold, he should be hit twice with the switch on the less sensitive parts of the body. Now the helper should stand still and the dog should release his hold. The handler must stand still for approximately thirty seconds without giving the dog any help whatsoever. When directed by the judge, he must proceed to make a search and disarm the helper. If the dog bites and does not release, the handler must go to his dog quickly and take him off. After this, follows a side transport to the judge, who will be approximately forty to fifty paces away. The handler must leave the examination area with his dog at heel.

6. Fighting Instinct (Courage and Hardness) (10 points)
The judge will carefully observe the dog's total performance in protection to evaluate his fighting instinct. The forging towards the helper and hard biting are some of the signs of the dog's fighting instinct. Should the dog try to avoid blows, he should immediately renew the attack on his own. Should the dog during the courage test return to the handler, or stay close to the helper without watching him, he can only receive partial credit. Full points for the fighting instinct can only be given to dogs who demonstrate exceptional courage and hardness.

Explanation: The command 'Leave' is in all phases allowed only once. Dogs who bite again after the leave command is given, or those who will not let go properly, can be penalized by up to fifteen points. Dogs who do not let go in all phases cannot receive the Schutzhund Degree. The helper does not have to stand motionless if it is necessary to move in order to see the dog, but in no circumstances should he make threatening motions. He should always protect himself and only stand completely motionless if the dog stands waiting in front of him. Only the energetic attacking and hard-biting dog who releases immediately after one command should receive full points. The dog who bites hard, but only releases after several commands, will lose up to five points. To get the dog off, commands other than 'Leave' are not permissible.

Note: If the dog has passed the temperament test prior to the examination, but later shows obvious signs of unsoundness, he may be excused from the examination.

General Information about Tracking

We should first differentiate between the trackingsolid, trackingsure and trackingclean dog.

The trackingsolid dog tracks by following the scent of the track, not the body scent of the track-layer. He should not search using air scent (as in the case in protection revere). We should also be aware that the scent track is not necessarily the same as the visual track. For example, if the wind is blowing across the trail, the dog will track more or less off to one side, not always at the same distance from the visual trail, depending upon the condition of the tracking area and the changing wind. The drive of the dog to follow the scent track is especially apparent when he overshoots the corners. This is not a fault since the wind actually carries the scent over the corners. But now let us see if the dog will attempt to find the tracking scent again, or will he begin to search. Since the trackingsolid dog has not yet learned to stay with the original scent, he will change over to other fresher tracks.

The trackingsure dog should stay with the original scent and should not change over to older or newer tracks. He has learned to distinguish between conflicting scents. The trackingsure dog is capable of differentiating if the age of the scent differs by three to five minutes. If the age difference between the tracks is less than three minutes, even the trackingsure dog will change over.

The trackingclean dog will remain with the original track regardless of the age of the scents.

Tracking Dog Examination

Requirements for admission:
Minimum age for the tracking degree (FH) is sixteen months.

Dogs who do not possess an SchH 1 degree can be entered in FH. However, the degree for Traffic-Proof Companion Dog (VB) must be in evidence. In this instance the degree will not be valid under the Breed-Show-Survey Regulations of the pure-bred dog breeding organizations.

Achievement in Tracking (100 points)   **Command**: 'Seek'
The track will be at least 1,500 paces long and at least three hours old. It will have six angles and three misleading tracks. Four articles will be dropped at different points on the track. So-called search packages will not be allowed. The dog will have to find the articles and pick them up or point them out as indicated by the handler to the judge before the exercise begins. It is the handler's prerogative to have his dog track free or on a 30-foot (10-metre) tracking leash. The line is not allowed to drag behind the dog.

Explanation: The track-layer has to be a stranger to the dog. The judge will hand the track-layer a sketch of the tracking area. The judge will sketch the route of the track, sign prominent markers, such as a lone tree, telephone post or large rock, and so on. The track-layer will show the four articles to the judge before laying the track. It is necessary that the track-layer has the four articles for at least thirty minutes before laying the track. The articles should be no larger than a wallet and should be of neutral colour.

At the start of the track, the track-layer will trample the ground over an area of one square yard (metre). He should then stand for approximately one minute, after which he will proceed, at a normal pace, to lay the track. The start of the track should be marked with an indicator. If possible, the start of the track should be at a house or cabin, because this simulates the real situation. The articles have to be dropped on the track at different intervals. The first article should be no closer than 250 paces from the start of the track. The fourth and last article will be dropped at the end of the track.

Dropping the articles at or close to a corner is not allowed. The articles should be dropped directly on the track, not beside it. The track-layer will mark the sketch whenever he drops an article. The track should be laid over varied types of terrain and over a well-used roadway. The track should be laid as it would be laid in a real situation, with a precise pattern being avoided.

Thirty minutes after the track is laid, a second person, strange to the dog, will be instructed by the judge to cross the track at three different places.

Atze tracking (SchH III).

The dog should pick up the scent at the start of the track, if possible without any influence from the handler. In no circumstances should the direction of the track be indicated to the dog by the handler. If the handler should feel that his dog has not picked up the scent, he will be allowed to start over again if the dog has not gone more than fifteen steps. For this, he will lose four or five points. The track should be worked out so that the handler can follow his dog at a walking pace. The pointing out may be done by sitting, lying down or standing. The handler must go to his dog immediately and take the article. The handler will praise his dog and continue on the track immediately. If the dog should find an article not belonging to the track-layer, he should ignore it. If the dog should follow one of the misleading tracks for more than twenty-five paces, the tracking should be stopped at that time.

Scoring: The dog is entitled to receive the full one hundred points, only if he worked the track at a nice steady pace and was able to find all four articles. All corners must be worked in a sure and confident manner. The dog should not be influenced by the misleading tracks and seven points will be lost for every missed article. The dog must pick up

144

or point out the article; to do both is faulty. Four points will be lost for every mistakenly picked up or pointed out article.

The Tracking Degree (FH) can only be awarded to the dog who receives a minimum of seventy points.

The following scores will be awarded:

0–35 points	–	Unsatisfactory
36–69 points	–	Insufficient
70–79 points	–	Satisfactory
80–89 points	–	Good
90–95 points	–	Very Good
96–100 points	–	Excellent

7

Showing and Judging

It is quite amazing how this sport has grown over a very short time, not only in the UK and USA, but in most countries that hold regular dog shows.

When I first started dog showing in the 1960s, entries, even at Championship Shows, were quite small, a total of forty dogs would be considered a fair entry, and one or two dogs in a class was not unusual. The withholding of first prize was quite common, since a first prize winner at a Championship Show in most classes qualified the dogs for Crufts and no judge wished to qualify a bad animal for the most prestigious dog show of the year.

The notion that the judge is out there to award prizes like sweeties to children should not be encouraged. Dog showing is a serious business, not only time consuming but expensive. The animal presented to the judge often represents many years of hard work for the breeder and it is the judge's job to evaluate and give opinion honestly, with no fear or favour.

Judges who do not measure up to this standard should not be supported but, unfortunately, it has been my experience over the years that the reverse is true. Some very erratic judging attempts have been rewarded at the next show with a larger entry. At every show, one sees dogs entered who are not prize winning specimens: they probably have several obvious and bad construction faults, or for one reason or another, lack breed type. This is where an irregular judge pulls the extra entry. Instead of singing the praises of these huge entries at shows, perhaps one must regard a huge entry with a little suspicion.

Overseas judges always draw a good entry. Perhaps exhibitors feel they may stand a chance under someone with a fresh outlook. Many newcomers bemoan the fact that several well-known people consistently win major honours. Their frustration is sometimes vented by accusing judges of face judging, meaning that the handler is either a well-known handler or well known to the judge. But it should be remembered that all well-known handlers started somewhere. The first time they en-

*Ch. Rottsann Classic Centurian, winning the group at Crufts
1986 (the only Rottweiler to have achieved this). Owned by
Mr Bromley.*

147

Baiting from the front – British style.

tered the ring they were also unknown, but have achieved their success by hard work, producing high-class stock.

Many newcomers to the ring think that showing is easy and that they should achieve quite quickly, which sometimes they do – only to be knocked back at the next show. Dog showing is a great leveller. The well-known handlers have all been through this before and take it in their stride. If their dogs are defeated, they melt away unnoticed, bench their dogs and get on with it. There is nothing to be achieved by throwing a tantrum. This is another lesson that has to be learned along the way. Most of the handlers who are now at the top have found to their cost and possibly embarrassment that it does not pay to accost the judge after he has finished judging and ask why they did not win. It is so unprofessional and childish, if not ill-mannered. You are there simply for the judge's opinion; if you cannot accept his opinion, it would perhaps be better if you didn't show.

Over the years, I have seen many truly nice people twisted by dog showing. They somehow take the judge's placements as personal, which they are obviously not. Just because someone does not think your dog is the greatest, it does not automatically follow that he has a

Side-stacking – Australian style.

personal dislike of you yourself. The judge is there to place the exhibits in order of merit. He does this to the best of his ability. Some do it better than others but, at all times, the judge's opinion must be accepted.

The Day of the Show

Preparations need to be undertaken several days before the show. A check of leads and equipment is the most obvious. Never go into the ring with grubby equipment. Leather leads should be treated with tack cleaning aids like saddle soap. Check chains should be in good condition: any with flaking chrome or worn rings should be discarded. If you want to bath your dog prior to the show, this should be done two days

Challenge Certificate.

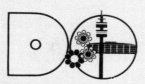

EUROPASIEGER-ZUCHTSCHAU DORTMUND '86
Für Hunde aller Rassen mit CACIB der FCI

URKUNDE

Verband für das Deutsche Hundewesen e.V.
Mitglied der Fédération Cynologique International

Name   Eika vom Barrenstein

Rasse   ROTTWEILER   ZB.-Nr. 65239

im Besitz von   Schnorr, Franz

erreichte die Formwertnote   Sehr gut 1   1588

Die Bewertung erfolgte durch einen international
anerkannten Zuchtrichter

Der Zuchtschauleiter

Dortmund, den 3. und 4. Mai 1986

Prize card from the European Show.

before, since the day after a bath, the coat tends to stand on end. It has been found that bathing black dogs with a shampoo that is recommended for dandruff not only clears any dandruff in the dog, but also makes black dogs seem even blacker.

If you use bait in the ring, it is advisable not to feed the dog the day before the show. This fasting not only makes the eyes appear brighter and coat look shinier, but also puts an edge on the appetite of the dog, thus making him more alert in the show ring. It is advisable to prepare your own bait. In the UK, this usually means liver, which can be boiled, diced and laid out on a tray in the oven where it dries out. This avoids a sticky mess on your fingers.

When travelling to shows, it is advisable to take your own water. A change of water can often upset a dog. When travelling to the show, always plan to arrive in good time. There is nothing worse than getting to a show and then having to rush straight into the ring. It is advisable to arrive a good hour before you are due to go into your class. When attending shows a long way from home, if this means setting off the day before and finding lodgings near to the showground, then this would be a better plan than starting out very early in the morning. In the United States, Australia and South Africa, sometimes it means starting

Showing your dog's teeth.

out several days before the show to arrive on time. In the UK it is possible to drive from one end of the country to the other in one day, although it is not ideal. Most Championship Shows have a dinner and a dance the night before the show starts. These are very good social occasions, if you like that sort of thing, and many people do.

If you have never exhibited a dog before, it is better to go to the show just to watch and study ring procedure. The fear of making a fool of oneself haunts many people and can ruin their chances in the ring. When I first started showing, I made a study of the most successful handlers and built my style on theirs. In the USA most of the dogs, if not all, are handled by professional handlers. There are a few professional handlers in the UK who have chanced their arm with Rottweilers, but up until the time of writing, none have been very successful. Showing in the UK, Scandinavia, Australasia, South Africa and the Caribbean is purely amateur in status, with owner handlers possibly making up at least 80 per cent of exhibitors.

The majority of the best handlers, though not all, train at All Breed Show handling classes. This is not only an excellent way to learn ring procedure, it is also good to socialize your Rottweilers with other breeds and have them handled by complete strangers. The advice one gets at such clubs is valuable, but not always accurate. For instance, you may be taught to handle by a Golden Retriever exhibitor, which would not get you very far in the show ring. So it is essential for you to know how to stack your dog.

Equipment Needed for the Show

- collar
- lead
- check chain
- bench chain
- blanket
- towel
- exhibit number pin
- stiff bristle brush
- soft bristle brush
- chamois leather
- coat spray
- bait (liver)
- water carrier
- blunt-nosed scissors

Judging

I am always amazed at the number of people who want to judge despite the fact that judging entails long journeys and inconvenience, long stints in the hot sun and driving rains, working long and hard. Is it a search for power or is it just very flattering to be asked to officiate?

Whatever the reason I maintain that no one should judge unless he has seen at least ten active years in the breed and had at least one very good dog. It is said that good judges are born to the job: they have a natural eye, a natural ability to assess quality and balance. Totally absorbed in the breed, they are generally concerned for the welfare and development of the breed mentally and physically. A good judge makes hard decisions decisively without making silly attempts to placate the defeated dog. Exhibitors appreciate this. If they are to be beaten, they would rather it happen with a clear decision than to see the judge walking from one dog to the other, clearly uncertain and under great stress. Judges lend their knowledge, unbiased and clear.

Each judge has a standing in the breed. Some who have had great dogs in the past are regarded with greater esteem than those whose grounding as a judge is less obvious. The only way to maintain our

The author with his Best in Show at the Bicentenary Club Show of Victoria 1988, Australian Ch. Anderjays our Marcus.

154

breed as we would want is to keep the judging at its highest standard; judges whose prowess is obviously lacking should not have their opinions sought by exhibitors.

A lifetime in the breed is not an automatic passport to judging. It is unfortunate that some people never seem to develop an eye, which is sad. It is only when you have developed a judging eye that you realize how little you know as a 'rookie'. If a judging career is embarked on too soon, you only make yourself look foolish. Putting up the dogs you saw at the last show is just fooling yourself and wasting everyone's time. A judge should not be influenced by previous performances in the show-ring. He should make his decisions on what he actually sees in the ring on the day. Many a judge is influenced subconsciously. How he deals with this is his own concern. What is important is to have a clear mind and get totally absorbed with the entry. Faced with the big winner in the class, a rookie judge must use his own opinion and totally reassess the animal with no preconceived views, placing the dog in the position he deserves and no more.

Some judges like to knock the winners, for no other reason that to prove they are impartial. This is just as bad, if not worse, than putting a dog up because of his previous record. This kind of judging is sometimes used for an ulterior motive: it is found that it produces a large entry for the judge's next appointment. Owners with the most moderate dogs feel they have a chance, because the judge never puts up the top winners. This kind of judge soon frightens off all the good dogs, the end result being that he deprives himself of a great deal of pleasure.

Some stud dog owners are often criticized for judging their own progeny too generously. I feel that if someone has laboured for many years to produce a type, it is hard not to recognize this type when it appears in the ring. However, this can go too far and other exhibitors will become exasperated. It is one thing to appreciate your own type, but the efforts of other breeders must be given equal time and evaluation. This kind of judging taken to its limits is known as kennel blindness.

Opinions differ, even amongst the best judges. This is what keeps us all going. It is the thrill of the uncertainty that keeps dog showing alive. Aspiring judges should counsel the best breeders and exhibitors. There are many contradictions, even at the highest level. Only by studying and absorbing different points of view can you come to your own opinion. Even after years of judging at the top, you will still have your misgivings and doubts. No animal is faultless, no judge infallible. Always stand by your opinions.

Ring presence catches everyone's eye.

Ring Procedure

A judge must be smart, without being eccentric in fashion. Clothes that do not flap about in the wind are the best. Large rings or bracelets can be a problem, I have seen several dogs ruined in the show ring by thoughtless or vain judges wearing jewellery which snared in the dog's mouth. It is the dogs that people have come to see, not the judge's fashion sense.

On arriving at the ring, the judge should first introduce himself to his steward and then plan his ring: where he wants the dogs to be examined, to stand and where he wants the examined dogs to stand. In the UK dogs will stand around the perimeter of the ring and the judge will then walk around the ring to gain his first impressions of the class. Many first impressions prove to be right. However, a judge should give plenty of time to get a general impression, especially of a very large class. It is easy for a very good dog to get lost with a novice handler.

The judge will then ask the class to move around the ring at the trot. Any lame dog should be noted and discarded. The reason for lameness

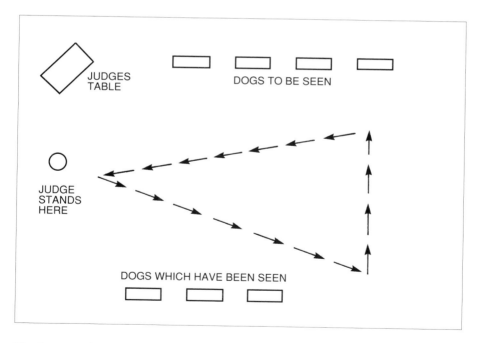

The dog moves in a triangle then straight up and down.

A judge assesses movement.

is not the concern of the judge: he is there purely to place them in order of merit. The number of times a judge sends the dogs round the ring is a matter for him. It will depend, however, on the class. Once or twice round the ring is quite enough for puppies, while a more searching test is appropriate for the open class.

The judge will then assess the exhibits individually, inspecting teeth, eye colour, condition, type, conformation and movement, and so on. The judge will then move the exhibits individually, firstly in a triangle and then once up and down. This gives him a view of the exhibit's movement from all angles.

While assessing the movement, the judge will firstly ascertain whether the exhibit is sound. Secondly, he will look for movement which is free and extended. A good mover moves his whole shoulders, has slight elevation and full extension of the whole foreleg. The reach should be enough to allow the pad to strike the ground first, the best angle for the shoulder blade is 45 degrees. This angle is assessed at the time of individual inspection by the judge.

Movement that is not desirable is described commonly as plaiting, pounding, padding, dishing and crabbing. Plaiting is when an exhibit places a forefoot in front of the other at the walk or trot; puppies do it due to vigorous growth or weakness. Most tend to grow out of it. A

The trot. Note the full extension.

judge should be careful not to fault an exhibit whose handler leans across and encourages him to look towards the handler's face since this will result in a dog's front legs crossing.

A dog's pad strikes the ground at full extension, but if this is not the case a dog will have unused momentum which has to go somewhere. The front assembly will absorb it like a shock absorber. This is known as pounding. A dog sometimes lifts his leg a little higher and holds it in suspension, hackney style. This movement is sometimes admired by the less knowledgeable ringsiders.

Crabbing is probably the most common movement fault. Because of interference from the hind feet crashing into the front, the dog finds it easier to turn his body a little to the side, usually head to the right and tail to the left. This allows the rear feet to drop without interference. This crab-like movement is a sure sign of poor construction.

Dishing is when the front feet flick out sideways. It is a different way of accommodating the same constructional fault that causes crabbing.

Conformation

It is known that in the middle of the first century AD a Roman agriculturist called Columella instructed all forty-day-old puppies to have

159

their tails bitten off to protect them from rabies. Docking is much older than some chronologists first thought. We can therefore summarise that the ancestors of the Rottweiler were the first docked around this time. Docking is not perhaps a purely German idea, but originated much further back in prehistory. Whatever the origins, we must appreciate that the breed has been bred to be balanced without a tail for thousands of years.

There are two kinds of conformation: static, when the dog is stationary; and kinetic, when he is on the move. Both forms must be present to form an overall picture of balance and so in one respect they are the same.

Angulation is the first aspect of conformation. The dog is in fact jacked around the ring by a series of levers and although many aspiring judges may not be aspiring engineers, the laws of leverage are as important to a show judge as they are to an engineer. Angulation is the angle formed by the bones of the front and rear assembly. The way these angles conform to the required standard as a whole is what interests us.

The Rottweiler is a stocky dog, compact and giving the impression

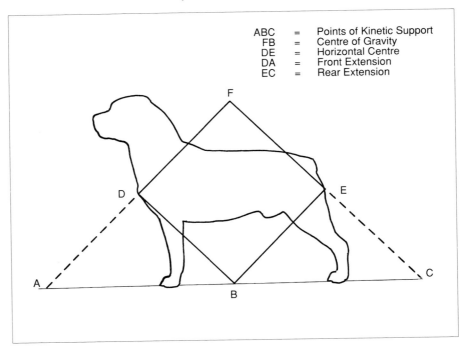

ABC	=	Points of Kinetic Support
FB	=	Centre of Gravity
DE	=	Horizontal Centre
DA	=	Front Extension
EC	=	Rear Extension

Balance.

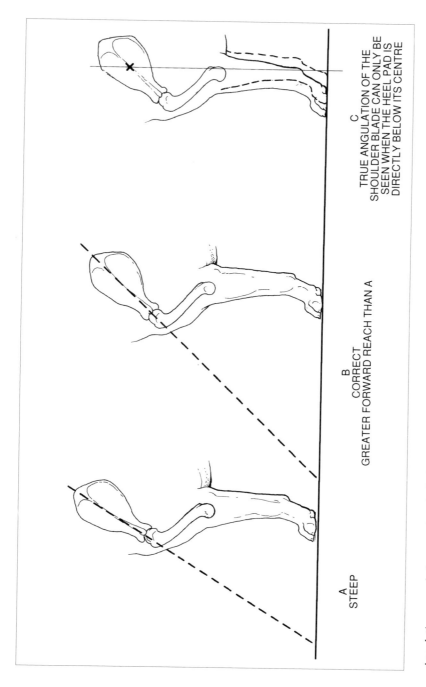

A
STEEP

B
CORRECT
GREATER FORWARD REACH THAN A

C
TRUE ANGULATION OF THE
SHOULDER BLADE CAN ONLY BE
SEEN WHEN THE HEEL PAD IS
DIRECTLY BELOW ITS CENTRE

Angulation can only be seen when the heel pad is directly beneath the centre of the shoulder blade. The impression of a good shoulder is given in (c), but this is false. The shoulder has rotated back with the forward movement of the legs.

of power while retaining manoeuvrability. All things are relative. A dog with a very powerful forehead and a very weak rear is in worse physical condition than a dog who is average throughout. It is very hard to generalize and I have seen many judges try. Questioned by exhibitors or owners as to what they were looking for when they judged, the obvious answer was the one that was closest to the Breed Standard, but sometimes judges are pressed to state whether they would prefer a good head to larger bone, or stronger hocks to well-angulated shoulders. These questions cannot be answered and really should never arise. The overall picture should be what counts for the most. I have seen many a great champion with a glaring fault and have seen many a mundane dog with no apparent faults at all. The charlatans of the show world always point to the great dog's fault, with never a reference to his outstanding merit. However, there is little point in placing a dog with a weak forehand even though he has the best and most powerful rear action ever seen, simply because he would not be able to absorb the hind thrust generated.

All things must balance; all pieces must fit. A great dog will always be obvious even to a novice. I have seen people with no breed experience at all pick out the good dogs in a class. They don't know how they do it; it just comes naturally.

The owner who has acquired a naturally balanced Rottweiler is very fortunate and particularly so in the case of a puppy. Some puppies stay balanced, even from a very early age, while others go through grotesque contortions during the growth stages. No Rottweiler can be really regarded as a good specimen unless he is balanced, statically and kinetically. Correct exercise can most certainly improve, if not completely achieve balance, in an animal not born with it, even though, as I have said, natural balance is a tremendous asset.

Balanced Front   As with the overall picture, individual fronts must also be balanced. The centre of gravity in the front assembly will be upward of the centre of the shoulder blade. For assessment of balance, the heel of the pad must be placed directly on this vertical line. If the heel is behind or in front of this central line, it alters the position of the shoulder blade. If it is in front of the line of gravity, it gives an impression of greater angulation of the shoulder blade, fooling the less knowledgeable.

The Front Assembly   As we have said before, the angulation of the shoulder blade is very important, not only to the balance, but the

162

forward extension, and therefore kinetic balance. This fact is appreciated by most judges. What is not understood so fully is the effect of the length of the humerus (or upper arm) on the power derived from the front assembly and equally, its ability to absorb shock. The longer the length of the humerus, the longer the length of the muscles attached to it and the shoulder blade. If the humerus has an angle of as much as 90 degrees from the shoulder blade, this is the most efficient means of increasing its length, the humerus and the shoulder-blade thus forming a right-angled triangle with two equal sides. A dog with this correct formation of the front assembly has pasterns which slope slightly forward. This is to maintain kinetic balance.

The Breed Standard states that feet should be strong, round, compact, with toes well arched, the hind feet being somewhat longer than the front. For myself, I have found the reverse to be true on a good specimen. Very often, we find that the rear feet are smaller and more compact than the front. Large hind feet are usually found on animals

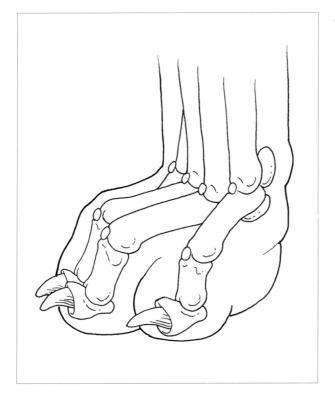

Anatomy of a correct foot.

that need a fast turn of speed, but for our breed, I would humbly suggest endurance is the main factor.

A smaller compact cat-like foot is seen on the majority of working dogs, simply because it is found that this type of foot conserves energy, is more robust and is less susceptible to injury. The main difference between the cat foot and the hare type foot is the dissimilarity in the length of the third digital bone. Lengthening the third digit increases the leverage action and therefore the speed. With a cat foot, you would get less speed but far more endurance.

Condition and appearance of the pads are very important to the dog, our breed in particular, because of the weight he carries. The pad must be thick and well built up, so that it is able to withstand more shock and rough treatment. Poor feet should never be tolerated by a judge. Thin pads and splayed feet or broken down pasterns should be instantly dismissed. There is a saying in the horse world which applies to dogs just as accurately: 'no foot, no horse'.

Dew-claws on the front legs are generally removed in the UK but not in Germany. It is interesting to note that wild dogs do not have rear dew-claws. Planned breeding has obviously reversed evolution to a

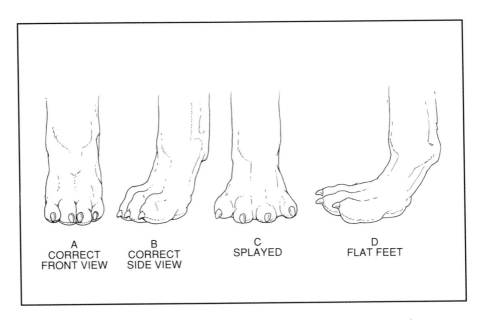

The foot. From left to right: (a) front view of correct foot; (b) side view of correct foot; (c) front view of incorrect, splayed foot; (d) side view of same fault.

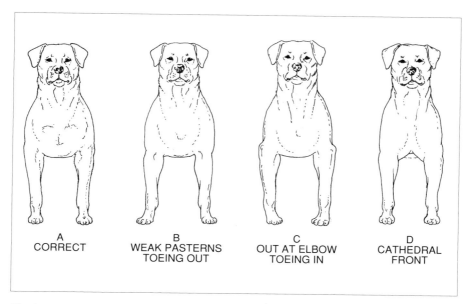

A	B	C	D
CORRECT	WEAK PASTERNS TOEING OUT	OUT AT ELBOW TOEING IN	CATHEDRAL FRONT

The front.

certain extent because front and rear dew-claws were used by the dog in the early stages of evolution to assist in climbing. The dog lost the ability to climb when speed became necessary in the hunt, thus encouraging the dog to specialize as a runner. Rear dew-claws are never found on the dingo or the wolf. However, it is sometimes found that even double dew-claws appear on some Rottweilers of certain strain. Littermates can vary from having double dew-claws to having none at all.

The Rear Assembly   The power or force generated by the back leg is passed through the centre of gravity towards the front assembly. The front assembly is always trying to maintain normal balance, while the rear is continually upsetting this balance with the power that it generates.

The correct angulation for our own breed and most working dogs is where the pelvic bone slopes off at an angle of 30 degrees. The ideal angulation for the femur is always 45 degrees to the ground. This encourages maximum length for the muscles which are attached to it. Consequently, the tibia and fibula are also of a longer length, giving us the hock, which is short and low set to the ground. The longer the hock, the faster the speed, as is the case in a rabbit or a hare. However, the longer the hock, the less endurance. As we are continually being told, our dog should be the type that can work all day. A dog with long hocks would never be able to accomplish this. The actual power generated by a hind leg can only be the difference between its contracted and expanded length. Unlike the front assembly, the back leg is actually attached to the spinal column, through which it transmits power to the front assembly.

Great importance is attached to the angulation of the croup. The croup must neither be too flat nor too angulated. Too much angulation, say 45 degrees, would produce what is known as a goose-rumped animal, 'all falling off at the croup', as many judges like to say. The actual degree of fall-off when looking at the dog is not actually 30 degrees because of the muscle and body attached to it. The actual fall-off in topline would be around 10–15 degrees. A flat croup would increase the length by an action. Sometimes when a dog actually throws his legs in all directions behind him, it is as a direct result of having a flat croup. There is no stop to the end of his hind thrust, so relatively speaking he could kick his legs almost vertically behind him, wasting vast amounts

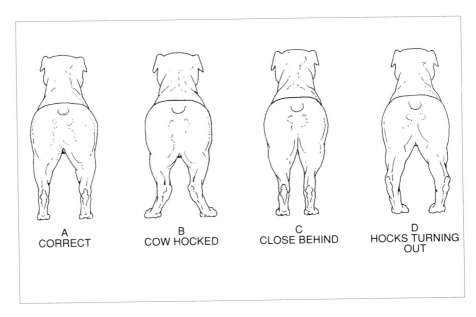

The back.

of power and energy. The goose-rumped dog has exactly the opposite problem; his length of rear extension is inhibited because the rear extension can only be drawn in a line with the angulation of the pelvic bone. A dog with a goose rump scuttles across the ring with a very short mincing stride. Both of these extremes in the angulation of the pelvic bone produce an ungainly action, which is easy to spot by the judge.

The upper thigh should not be too short. It should be broad and strongly muscled. The only way to achieve this is by having a femur with a 45 degree angle to the ground. This is common in most breeds. By having this particular angle, we have the longest possible length from A to B.

The lower thigh should be well muscled at the top and strong and sinewy lower down. With a long tibia and fibula, the muscles in this area have extra length and strength, therefore providing the well-bent stifle that we are looking for. The extra length of the tibia and fibula will also provide us with a long Achilles tendon and the muscles that activate the hock, a most important function of the entire assembly.

Hocks generally are not perfectly straight, but bent slightly forward. This again is to provide a centre of balance pivot, exactly below the centre point of gravity. A dog whose hocks bend too far forward is described as being 'sickle-hocked'. Dogs who are over-angulated in the stifle joint also tend to be sickle-hocked in order to put the pad at the best possible point for balance. The hocks, when viewed from the rear when the dog is standing, should turn neither in nor out. If they do turn in, the dog is said to be 'cow-hocked'. Many puppies start their lives being cow-hocked, but grow out of it with maturity. I have very rarely seen a Rottweiler turn his hocks out, but this is generally associated with having slack loins or weak muscle tone. Hocks in this position have the effect of making the dog look pigeon-toed.

Body Length Body length for the Rottweiler should be as 9 is to 10. People who have worked it out on computer assure me that a 9:10 dog should appear square. If that is the case, most Rottweilers are more than 9:10. If a dog is overlong, he is said to be long in back although this is not always the case - he is possibly long in loin. The Breed Standard uses the word 'compact'. A dog that is long in loin could never look compact. However, a dog that is well-ribbed up, with a deep roomy chest and well-sprung ribs, with very little tuck-up, even though he would exceed the 9:10 ratio, would still look compact. Dogs that are too compact often have the problem of the back feet over-reaching and touching the front feet, making the dog crab or plait.

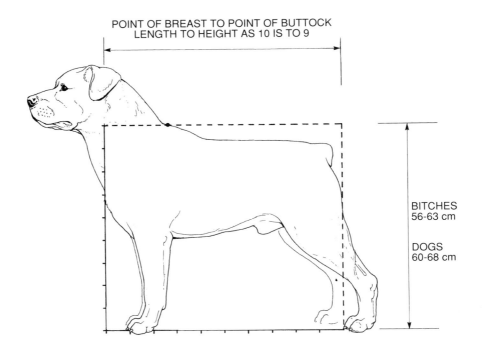

POINT OF BREAST TO POINT OF BUTTOCK
LENGTH TO HEIGHT AS 10 IS TO 9

BITCHES
56-63 cm

DOGS
60-68 cm

Desired proportions for the Rottweiler.

Just one point of extra length in back avoids all these problems. Perhaps this is why German breeders are at the moment preferring a dog that is slightly longer than we would usually see in the UK or the USA.

Length of neck plays a big part in the overall balance and effect. The neck should be strong, slightly arched, of a good length and be round and very muscular. Dogs with short, stubby necks will never look balanced.

A judge should never fault-judge. If a dog does have a fault, to point to the dog's one fault is not really judging. However, having said this, there are faults that should never be tolerated.

The Head   Head quality is most important in the Rottweiler. Some judges in fact are known as head judges. They are unable to see a dog unless it has a good head.

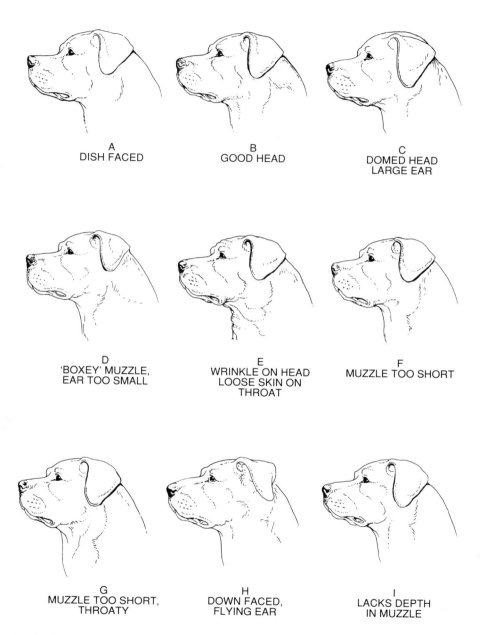

A
DISH FACED

B
GOOD HEAD

C
DOMED HEAD
LARGE EAR

D
'BOXEY' MUZZLE,
EAR TOO SMALL

E
WRINKLE ON HEAD
LOOSE SKIN ON
THROAT

F
MUZZLE TOO SHORT

G
MUZZLE TOO SHORT,
THROATY

H
DOWN FACED,
FLYING EAR

I
LACKS DEPTH
IN MUZZLE

The head.

Rottweiler heads must be dry, by which it is meant that there must be no loose skin. This is a fault that has taken many years to breed out and must not be allowed to creep back in. Not only the skin on the head, but also that on the throat must be tight.

The best Rottweiler heads give an appearance. The skull between the ears should be broad, but not domed, with the occipital bone well developed but not conspicuous. The cheeks, or filling under the eyes, known as the zygomatic arch, is well formed. If this is not the case, the head will always appear plain. The muzzle should be deep, with the topline level and the length not longer than the length from the stop to the occiput. The powerful head and jaws of the Rottweiler are two of the features of the breed, and contribute much to breed type. The importance of the head cannot be underestimated.

The nose is always black and well developed, with large nostrils. The eyes should be of medium size in proportion to the head, almond shaped but not too narrow. There has been a tendency in Germany in recent years to breed a rounder eye than we would normally see. The explanation for this is that instances of entropion are far less frequent with a rounder eye. I think one of the problems we have caused ourselves in the past is the misinterpretation of the almond-shaped eye. Deep narrow eyes have been accepted as almond-shaped, which is not the true interpretation. Eyes that are slightly rounder than almond should not be penalized. Colour varies from dark amber to dark brown. Bright yellow eyes and black eyes are not encouraged. However, I have never seen a black eye penalized.

Untidy ears will always spoil the overall impression of an otherwise excellent head. Rottweiler ears are always pendant, small in proportion to the head, although recently the German Club has decreed that they should be slightly larger in size, but this must not be taken to mean that large ears are required. It is just a statement to clarify that ears were getting too small, thus causing the problem of 'flying ears', or 'rose' ears. They are set high on the head and wide apart and lie flat across the cheek and should not be too thin.

When examining the teeth, I maintain that the judge should always ask the exhibitor to show the teeth, because in handling more than one exhibit's mouth, the judge is in a position to pass infection from one mouth to another. If one of the first exhibits of the day has a contagious disease, it can be spread to the entire entry by the end of the day. Some judges like to prove how fearless they are by diving in and handling every dog themselves. It is not the judge's job to show the dog; it is the handler's and he will know the best way to approach his own dog. The judge tells the handler exactly what he wants to see, usually the bite first, then the left side, then the right side, to check for any missing teeth.

Coat   The coat is very important. It is not only functional, but also crucial to the aesthetic picture that we are trying to realize.

A Rottweiler with a short Dobermann-type coat can never be called typical of the breed. This one, some may say small, fault is not only hereditary, it seriously detracts from the typical visual aspect we are trying to conjure. Conversely, a dog who carries a long rough coat must be totally discarded, as this fault is also of an hereditary origin. Coats that appear wavy must be discouraged too and therefore penalized by the judge. A very slight wave can be tolerated on the rump. Wavy, coarse coats always spoil the look of even a quality animal.

Temperament   Dogs who show any temperament problem, either over-aggressiveness or shyness (i.e. will not be handled), should be discarded.

8
Breeding

The rise in popularity of the Rottweiler over the last few years has not been without its cost. Unfortunately, the breed, through over-breeding, became available to irresponsible people. Dogs have been kept in totally unsuitable homes by people who are uncaring and selfish, and who have no regard for the breed, their only God being money.

Before one embarks on a breeding programme, one should analyse the motive behind the desire to breed a litter of Rottweilers. If that desire is inspired or motivated by the quest for monetary gain, then breeding should not even be considered. Finding homes is relatively easy, if you are not too worried about the situation that the puppy will find itself in. But finding suitable homes where the animal will be loved, trained and cared for properly is very difficult.

Look at your bitch and ask yourself several questions. Is she good enough to be bred from and what would she contribute to the gene pool? Is she X-rayed? Hip dysplasia is a very common problem in Rottweilers and great strides have been made to eradicate this crippling disease. If someone breeds from a bitch without any thought or care, this could contribute a backward step in the fight against hip dysplasia and you may find one of your owners coming back in less than a year's time and being able to claim all his money back, because you did not take reasonable care with the selection of the sire or the dam of the puppy that he has purchased.

Is the bitch mentally sound? In these harrowing days where breeders are under a great deal of pressure in the UK and moves are afoot to ban the breed entirely, we must make sure that the basic breeding stock is of sound mental character. The only way to achieve this is to attend a character test run by an official Rottweiler club. The mental state and character of the sire of the puppies is of paramount importance, but the mental state and character of the brood bitch cannot be over-emphasized. The puppies will gain all their formative learning in the nest and a nervous bitch rears nervous puppies. Nervous puppies grow into nervous adults, fear biters, and so on.

The next question you may ask yourself is whether the bitch is free from all hereditary and inherited diseases. Entropion is one of the commonest, but there are many others. Again, anyone who buys a puppy from you and the puppy is then found to have inherited this extremely painful eye defect will be very angry that you did not take the necessary precautions to avoid this distressing condition.

Having assessed your bitch, you must now decide whether you are a suitable person to breed dogs. Have you got enough time? Rearing a litter of puppies is very hard work. It could not be accomplished by somebody who works nine to five. Puppies are fed four times a day when they are three to four weeks old and you must be able to do this. If you cannot, you really should forget about mating your bitch. It takes a special person with a genuine love for the breed, with the knowledge and understanding that only come with experience, to make what I call a real breeder. Of course, anyone can breed from a bitch and call themselves a breeder; it is one of the most open terms ever used. Breeding is an art, a feeling and a love.

True breeders are made in heaven, I feel, in much the same way as green-fingered gardeners. If asked to define their skill, they would be hard pressed to pin-point their success. It just comes naturally, they would tell you. Deciding which dog to mate to which bitch can involve an element of luck and sometimes does to a great extent. What cannot be put down to luck is the breeder who continues to produce top-class specimens time and time again, litter after litter. These are the real breeders and in most breeds they can be counted on one hand. Anyone starting out to emulate this type of breeder must set his foundations squarely, building on stock with no known hereditary faults and sound mental disposition.

Genetics

A basic understanding of genetics is important for any breeder, and since most other books on the breed have given genetics a wide berth, I feel I must grasp the nettle, even if I am only able to give a very simplified account of the subject.

Mendel's Theory of Heredity

Mendel was a monk and scientist, who through his experiments with peas, was able to establish what we know today as Mendel's law.

He was made Abbot in 1860 and for fifteen years taught biology in the monastery school, while at the same time making his own researches into heredity characteristics. He was in fact trying to record the reappearance of unit characters in successive generations. He achieved this by crossing two contrasting types of garden pea, the green seeded and the yellow seeded. He found that by crossing one variety with another (cross fertilization), he produced hybrids in which only one colour, yellow, appeared. Therefore, yellow was deemed to be the dominant and green the recessive character.

Mendel found by further cultivation that the offspring of his first crosses produced 25 per cent pure dominant (yellow) character, 25 per cent pure recessive (green) character, whilst the remaining 50 per cent were hybrid like their parents, with yellow still dominant and green recessive. Added to this, he discovered that the 25 per cent yellow reproduced only pure yellows and the 25 per cent green only pure greens.

Ch. Rottsann Regal Romance, JW., owned by Mrs Liz Dunhill. This bitch not only had a fantastic career, but proved to be prepotent as a brood bitch, becoming top UK Brood Bitch All Breeds 1990. She is sired by Jagen Blue Andante out of Rottsann Classic Crystal, both being Bulli descendants. [photo courtesy Mrs Dunhill]

Therefore, characteristics are either dominant or recessive. The offspring of the first generation inherit the dominant characteristics; the recessive characteristics lie dormant and appear in the second and later generations.

However, if two individuals possessing recessive characteristics mate, recessive character becomes dominant in their offspring. How often have we seen in a dog a fault such as long coat appear as if from nowhere, from parents with perfectly good coats? The temptation is always to blame the stud dog, but it must be that both parents are recessive long coats. The same principle applies to all genetic faults. This is why a good working knowledge of the pedigree of intended breeding dogs is essential. The counsel and experience of older respected breeders must be sought by inexperienced or first time breeders if they want to avoid mistakes in the genetic minefield.

A puppy will receive from its parents a collection of genes, which are arranged in groups like a string of beads. Each string is known as a chromosome. The chromosomes exist in the nucleus of each cell in the body. The number of chromosomes present in each nucleus is dictated by the species: human beings have forty-six, domestic dogs have seventy-eight. In ordinary cells, chromosomes are paired, two of each kind. Therefore dogs have thirty-nine pairs.

When the reproductive cells are formed, the pair separates so that each sperm or ovum contains only one of each pair of chromosomes. When a sperm fertilizes an ovum by uniting with it, the full seventy-eight chromosomes are restored, the offspring receiving one of each pair from each parent.

The genes are arranged in a definite order in the chromosomes, situated in the same place in corresponding chromosomes, all affecting the same characteristics but sometimes in different ways. They are then said to be allelic to each other. Different allelic forms are believed to have originated through chemical or physical changes which occur suddenly and are called mutations. Mutations are the basis of evolution, most are detrimental but a small number are beneficial to the species. Genes located at different places in the same chromosome are said to be linked, but do not necessarily all affect the same part of the dog.

When a dog has two different alleles at a certain place on corresponding chromosomes, they are said to be heterozygous for those genes. If the two genes of a pair are of the same kind, they are said to be homozygous.

Other technical terms which must be understood are genotype, which refers to the gene complex, or what is derived from the animal's parents; and phenotype which refers to the characteristics that can be seen in the dog itself, for instance, a badly fed dog will appear to be a poor specimen. Even if the dog's genes are of the first order, environment has a large part to play.

The idea that one gene has one effect is untrue. The effectiveness of any one gene depends on the whole inherited make-up of the animal. One gene may produce a pleasing characteristic, but this characteristic may be changed to a certain degree by the effect of a rival gene. For example, one gene may produce an excellent head shape, while another produces a beard, which is quite unacceptable in our breed, completely spoiling the appearance of an otherwise excellent head. When a certain gene is known to be able to produce its full effect, even in the presence of rival genes, it is said to be dominant if the rival is its allele, and epistatic if its rival is not its allele. Genes that can only produce an effect when present in duplicate are said to be recessive.

If black is dominant and white recessive, white will lie dormant in the offspring of the first generation. The progeny of the first generation will show pure white, pure black and black with white recessive.

Line-breeding is the most useful tool for the breeder. Line-breeding means producing puppies from lines where one or two outstanding individuals appear more than once. The blood of these outstanding individuals can only be held by in-breeding.

In-breeding should only be undertaken by knowledgeable people in the breed, from animals who are outstanding and with no apparent faults. As we have seen, faults can be recessive, which is why only experts with a working knowledge of the breed should attempt this most potent of breeding aids.

If the result of in-breeding should be disappointing, this does not condemn the parents, but points to the fact that a less close mating should be made.

Dogs who have faults that appear as a result of line-breeding should be culled or sold without papers. In this way, we cleanse our lines. Dogs who breed pure are retained, but when an individual is seen to produce bad genetic faults in his offspring, those animals, too, should be released from the breeding programme, along with his progeny.

The majority of newcomers to our breed have little knowledge of the dogs that appear in the pedigree of their dogs. This knowledge is hard to acquire, as breeders tend to be cagey about disclosing even slight faults while the animal is still alive or has an active stud life.

It must be remembered that dogs in the fifth generation only contribute 3.125 per cent of the inheritence of a pup. So, for the newer students of pedigree, a good knowledge of the first three or even four generations is all a breeder requires. It is more important to have a thorough knowledge of this area than it is to have a pedigree so long it could cover a wall!

If we find a negative side to a dog's pedigree, i.e. if the pedigree shows dogs who we feel, for some reason, could not contribute to the vision we have of what we want to produce, we must find a mate whose pedigree does not contain this individual or individuals, but does contain the common ancestors from the positive aspect of our pedigree, i.e. the dogs we admire or are told are good producers. This will in effect double or treble their contribution, while weakening the negative aspect considerably.

The formation of true breeding strain should be the ambition of every breeder. This cannot be achieved by buying a second-rate foundation bitch and mating it to the top winning dog of the moment. This may make economic sense, but it is a genetic disaster.

Common Defects and Diseases proved to be Hereditary

Abnormal Behaviour (shyness, fear, biting, etc)
Abnormal Behaviour (whirling, shadow chasing)
Dysplasia 'of the hip and elbow'
Ectropion (out-turned eyelids)
Entropion (in-turned eyelids)
Epilepsy (fits)
Glaucoma
Haemophilia
Kidney stones
Monorchidism and Cryptorchidism
Patella Luxation
Skin diseases
Teeth (missing)
Sterility
Tumours

Breeding a Litter

If you decide that all the things we have discussed previously are true and your bitch fulfils all the qualities we have outlined, your first consideration must be a suitable stud dog. As I have said before, the choice of a stud dog can be a matter of luck, or you may have seen favourable litters produced from bitches who have similar breeding to your own.

Champion dogs are not always the most suitable dogs to use merely because they are champions. High quality dogs do not always produce high quality puppies. One must look for a dog that actually produces high quality puppies. He may not be a champion himself, as was the case in the UK with Chesara Dark Herod who I do not think would have won many prizes in the show ring. However, due to the experience of his owner and his breeding, he was test mated and proved to sire high quality puppies, which he did with monotonous regularity. He was to achieve a status of Number 5 Top Stud Dog All Breeds, a great achievement for any Rottweiler, particularly one with no show record. This is a classic example of a dog who would not have been used, had it not been for the experience and knowledge of his owner, and a major influence on the breed in the UK would have been lost.

Choosing a stud dog is not an easy task. Therefore, it is wise to choose

Ch. Chesara Dark Charles, a great stock-getter. Owned by J. Elsden.

a stud dog with a proven track record, who has at least some ancestors, preferably at least a quarter of a pedigree, which is related in some way to the best dogs on your bitch's own pedigree. This keeps the gene pool tight, with not too much outcross. If none of the ancestors are related, you will have a very large gene pool and it is very unlikely that you will be able to forecast with any clarity the type of puppy that you will produce. Cutting down the gene pool is like cutting down the number of fruits on a fruit machine. If you have ten fruits on a one-armed bandit, it is much harder to get them in one line and win the big prize, but if you cut them down to just three, getting these fruits in one line is not such a difficult task. I tend to look at genetics in this way.

With our own breeding programme, we line-breed and try to outcross only to a very good dog with at least 25 per cent of the blood-lines we already have. This gives us hybrid vigour from the new blood-lines, without losing type.

Mating your Bitch

We have always found with our bitches that the eleventh day after the first sign of colour is the best. We have always mated our bitches on this day and have had very few disappointments.

As soon as your bitch shows colour, you should ring the stud dog owner and let him know that your bitch is in season and the date you expect her to be ready for mating. Ask the stud dog owner all the details that you require, such as the price of service, and so on, so that on the day, everything is ready and there are no hold-ups. The stud fee is usually paid on a tie, which means that if the dog ties with your bitch, you then pay a fee. We have never charged anyone for a slip mating, but I understand that some people do. If this produces a litter, fine; if not, the bitch's owner would be very disappointed. We find it advisable for the stud dog owner to take the risk and charge for service if a litter results from a slip mating.

To produce a good tie, it is necessary to make some simple explanation of the anatomy of the reproductive organs and the biological process of mating. Many people feel that mating is just a natural process and two dogs can accomplish this quite easily without any human factor. This may be true, but someone who has a very valuable stud dog is not prepared to let it run free in a field with a bitch, risking possible injury. Rottweilers are heavy dogs and very powerful. If a bitch took fright during the tie, it could very badly damage the male and the bitch herself. It is vital that there is an experienced person present during all matings.

After the bitch's trip to the dog, she should be walked, calmed down, patted and caressed. To a bitch, being mated for the first time can be very frightening. She should be introduced to the dog slowly, both male and female patted and stroked, hopefully taking all the tension out of the situation. The dog will be very keen. Bitches are usually reserved, although it is not uncommon to see a bitch whose sexual appetite is stronger than the dog's. Experienced bitches tend to stand rock still. It is ideal for a young dog to have a more experienced bitch for his first mating.

It is not uncommon for a bitch with a perfectly sound temperament to become very uneasy when she is being mated for the first time. She will try to get away. She will twist, roll over, even snap. I have been present at several matings where a bitch of this type was being pushed, pulled and shoved in all directions with the dog leaping over several people to try and accomplish his task. The two dogs were allowed to run free and the mating took place without any help. Sometimes this is the best way, sometimes not. You have to judge the reactions of the dogs to each other: what suits one bitch will not suit another. If the dogs are allowed to run free, it must be in a small confined area, where they are easily retrieved.

Once the dog has actually mounted the bitch, he will try to penetrate her vulva, which is the thickened fleshy orifice usually called the lips of the vagina. His penis is not enlarged at this stage. Upon contact with the vulva, he will make strong thrusting movements to penetrate. It is then that the penis and two bulbs, which form at the base of the penis, enlarge. The bulbs, when inside the female passage, become very swollen and lock the penis in a swollen condition into the female passage. This condition is known as a tie. It can last from thirty seconds to one hour. The size of the swollen bulb is quite remarkable. In our breed, the size of the bulbs on most dogs are about the size of two medium sized tomatoes. This is the most dangerous time for the dog and bitch, because the bitch will start to cry and may try to escape. This is also the time that the dog starts to pump seminal fluid, which contains spermatozoa, which are the male seed or sperm cells. As the dog pumps, you can usually see his tail twitch. Each twitch is one pump. This is also observed when a dog slip mates: every time he pumps a contraction can be seen under his tail. The slip mating is when the whole procedure that we have just discussed is gone through, but the dog slips out before he is able to lock into the bitch. The two bulbs

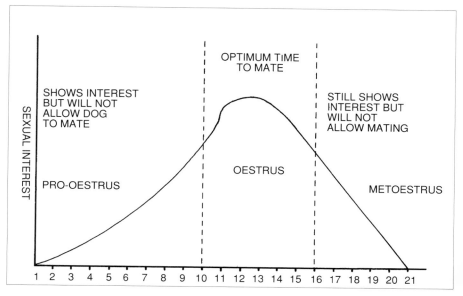

The normal oestrus cycle.

at the base of the penis are expanded and so the dog ejaculates into thin air. This can be quite distressing for him.

When to Mate

Firstly, you must make yourself aware of the time your bitch comes into season, usually every six months, although some bitches come in every four months. This is the first trip wire to negotiate. Bitches will usually drop their coat before coming into season, so this is a very good signal to watch for. Do not assume anything. Attention to detail is most important. We find that eleven days after the first sign of blood is the best time to mate the bitch. However, bitches may clean themselves constantly and it may mean you miss this first sign. This can be your second trip wire so allow for this. Have some white cotton wool available and dab it into the vulva daily. If it shows red, this is Day 1. Extra indications are a general swelling of the vulva, which usually grows to twice its usual size and becomes very spongey.

If you ring the stud dog owner and ask to use his or her stud dog when you are not sure of the day your bitch is due to be mated, it is reasonable to expect him to turn you down. The only way to gain a hint if you have missed all previous signs is to let another dog sniff your bitch and gauge his reaction. For this, you would need an experienced stud dog. Next door's mongrel would probably mate her at any stage of her cycle, so his opinion would be useless. Therefore, to find someone who would allow you access to their stud dog in the knowledge that it will upset him for the rest of the day would be very difficult. To safeguard against uncertainty, it is better to make a little effort.

So let us assume you have got the right day, your bitch is in full season and you are ready to go to the stud dog of your choice. Always start off in good time, allowing at least half an hour before you have arranged for the service. This gives the bitch time to settle, have a walk, take a drink and generally calm down. It is a very bad thing to take the bitch straight from your car to the stud dog. Not only will this frighten her, but she is probably feeling uncomfortable after the trip and it would be totally unreasonable of you to expect her to perform immediately.

Once she is totally relaxed, you can introduce her to the stud dog. Do not let the dog rush in and virtually rape her. This is not good for the bitch or the prospect of puppies. Let the dog lick her ears and generally show what a handsome brute he is! She will soon show some interest. Although she will still look sideways at you, make sure you reassure her by using her name and scratching her rump, which increases sexual arousal.

Stud dogs usually fall into different types: the dashing youngster who will give it all he has got, to no avail and only when he is virtually exhausted will he slow down and succeed almost without trying; the aggressive type who will grumble with impatience throughout and, only when the tie is successful, adopt a stupid grin of contentment; and the old hand who has seen it all before, who takes his time, is very methodical and very rarely fails. This last type of dog is wonderful if you have one. In my experience they are very rare.

Most matings are full of stress. I have seen married couples with a stud dog, who, in the general order of things, get on very well, but at mating times are totally at each other's throats and can be reduced to a blazing row in front of complete strangers, all because the dog will not perform. For my own part, I can only say that of all the duties involved in dog ownership, stud work is the least enjoyable, but I have found that a relaxed atmosphere does help immensely. There is no way that you can make a dog mate a bitch. There are many people who claim to be experts and will travel the length of the country to push and pull and squeeze. The best matings are natural matings, when both participants are relaxed and in a happy frame of mind. I realize that this is no consolation if you have driven hundreds of miles to use a particular dog only to find that he 'has a headache' in doggy terms. However, you must be patient and let things take their natural course. In general, Rottweilers are not difficult to mate.

Let us assume you have had a good tie. Then and only then is the stud fee payable. A stud fee is exactly that. It is not a puppy fee, by which I mean you do not pay for puppies. If no puppies are produced, it is not the fault of the stud dog, assuming he has already proven himself. However, most stud dog owners will allow you a free return if no puppies are produced, but this is not a right, it is just an unwritten rule. If the bitch misses for a second time, the stud dog owner may ask for a half stud fee for a third mating.

The Bitch's Age

We have always felt that a Rottweiler bitch needs to be at least two years old at the time of whelping. I know many people in the breed would not agree with me on this point, but I feel that there can be no justification for mating a bitch before this time. Rottweilers are easy to whelp, the whelp being comparatively small in comparison to the size of the bitch. Over the years, we have experienced very few whelping problems. Therefore, the old chestnut that a bitch should be mated so that she can whelp before her bones have set does not really hold much water. From my own experience, bitches who have been mated at a very early age, without exception, grow up to be very sullen adults, lacking character and self-esteem.

Producing puppies from an animal who is no more than a puppy herself, I feel cannot be a good thing, either for the puppies or the mentality of their mother. There is only one reason I can see for mating a bitch at an early age and that is monetary gain and I do not only blame the bitch owner. As they say, it takes two to tango and somewhere there is a stud dog owner who was prepared to let his dog be used; sometimes a mercenary stud dog owner actually encourages novice owners to mate their bitches, probably even before they would have thought of doing so. This type of person is to be despised for the harm they do. They usually charge a lower stud fee than anyone else to try to encourage as many people as possible to use their stud dog. Usually the dog is of a second rate nature possibly a good dog, but not top class. However, the slightly reduced stud fee may appeal to the uneducated but I can assure you it is false economy.

This leads us to the next conclusion. How many times should a dog be used at stud, once, twice, three times a week? How long is a piece of string? It is hard to say. Perhaps the dog may be used three times in a week. If he were, I would say that he should then be rested for some time before he is used again. The over-use of stud dogs is very counter-productive. In the short term, however, it makes the bank balance look very good. Someone who over-uses a stud dog, and I have heard extreme cases of a dog being used twice in one day, would ultimately lead to the shortening of the stud career for that individual dog.

As we shall see elsewhere in this book, some top-class specimens have never sired stock anywhere near the quality of themselves, where-as dogs who have not even made it to the show ring have become top sires. However, as a general rule of thumb, the show ring is the shop window and we assess the qualities of the future stud animals from this shop window, although it must be remembered that you cannot judge a book by looking at the cover. It is the quality of the progeny which will determine the ultimate standing of each stud dog.

Some stud dog owners may ask for a special arrangement at the time of mating. Possibly they want to take a puppy in lieu of stud fee or something along those lines. This type of breeding agreement is not unusual, but you must be very careful. If you are not sure, ask advice from a more experienced breeder. Basically, any breeding agreement must be written down. What was agreed at the specific time, even between friends, can be blurred by time and, even when it is written down, people sometimes interpret it differently. The problems caused by breeding agreements are legion and have caused the break-up of many long-standing friendships. I personally would strongly advise against any breeding agreement, unless you know the person par-ticularly well and even then, as I have said before, get it down in writing. This will save you a lot of heartache in the long run.

Having completed a successful mating, it is necessary for the stud dog owner to complete some paperwork. To enable you to register the puppies with the Kennel Club, it is necessary for the stud dog owner to sign the relevant forms. Most stud dog owners have these readily available, but it is always better to ask, and if they do not have any to hand, you must apply for them yourself. Always have one ready to be signed at the time of mating. This can be held as a receipt of mating.

When Things Go Wrong

You may arrive to mate your bitch and find that the dog or the bitch shows no interest. If all the signs indicate that the proper stage of oestrus has been reached, there are several things you can do. Either leave the bitch with the stud dog owner, or visit your vet who can carry out tests to determine what stage of oestrus the bitch is now at. Many bitches can indicate very strongly that they are ready to mate, even show positive signs and then may stand for a further ten days, at which time they may be mated and conceive quite happily. However this is unusual.

The aggressive bitch is usually the type who has been pampered or spoilt or treated as a substitute child. She does not really consider herself to be a dog and is terrified by this strange animal trying to mount her. Of all the different types of bitches we have had at the kennels, this type is the one I most dislike, having been bitten quite badly several times by bitches who, at home, are very loving, sociable animals. The aggression comes directly from fear. Usually, there is no way of convincing this bitch that this is the right thing to do, having been reared in such a way as to believe she is human. What one must do is muzzle the bitch because she can do not only damage to the handlers, but also put a young dog or an inexperienced dog off stud work for many weeks, if he receives a bite. The bitch must be restrained. The best way is to hold her by the collar, keeping her head forward and low. This has the effect of making it hard for her to sit down. Not only will you need support at the front, it is advisable for two people to lock hands beneath her tummy to give support there, because she will do her best to drop down. As soon as the dog penetrates, she will try to throw herself on the floor. With this many people around the bitch, it needs a very inexperienced dog not to climb on. This is certainly not the type of bitch to introduce to a young dog at his first mating.

Tall bitches may be difficult to penetrate for the average dog, while with a smaller bitch, the dog sometimes goes right over the top! In both cases, you have a problem of alignment. Some people either prepare a ramp, which I have never found to be successful, or a steep incline. If the bitch is too tall, she will face downhill; if she is a little short, she will face uphill, which will give you several inches difference in elevation.

Left to their own devices, dogs seem to be able to mate anything. We once had a Rottweiler at our kennels mate a Norwegian Buhund bitch, a little more than 14 inches (36cm) high. So it is not impossible. It just takes a little more time. When alignment is a problem, just draw back and look at the situation. Don't let the dog exhaust himself with fruitless pumping. The more he tires, the harder the problem becomes.

Another problem is the dog who shows interest, but will not mate. We have often had this problem with our well-known stud dog, Jagen Blue Andante. He would show great interest in the bitch, but would insist on marking his territory first, which meant a fairly lengthy job round the orchard, christening every tree, sniffing here and there, at first showing complete disinterest in the bitch. Sometimes, he would even take a dip in the pool if it was a bit hot! As you can imagine, this infuriated us, even though we had to keep our cool, while trying to reassure the bemused owner of the bitch. The way we used to counteract this would be to take the bitch back to the car. The dog would instantly think that she was being taken away and would dash back to mate her before she left. It seemed to work every time. The one thing Andante knew was that the bitch had come for him. He was a very experienced stud dog and would think to himself that he would do it in his own good time.

Andante, however, was a very particular dog. On many occasions, we had bitches brought to him who were showing all the obvious signs of being absolutely right for mating. However, he would not mate them. As you can imagine, the owners of these bitches were quite annoyed. We would always say to them that if Andante would not

Jagen Blue Andante, sire of many top winners.

mate the bitch, she was not ready, although this explanation did not always find favour with the bitch owner, who had probably travelled many hours to reach us. Several of these bitches whom he refused to mate were then taken on to other stud dogs, who did mate them. However, in every case, the bitch did not conceive. This gained Andante quite a reputation as a dog who would only mate when the bitch was right, and in view of this, many bitches who had previously missed many times were brought to stay here and we were able to make several observations. Some bitches actually come into season, go through the stages of oestrus and then, for some unapparent reason, go out of season and come in again in a week's time or even later, as I have said before. Andante mated a bitch on her twenty-eighth day of oestrus, to which she conceived and produced eleven puppies. He was, in fact, an exceptional stud dog and the mere fact that he was not over-eager proved to be a great asset, although sometimes a little frustrating. We had to learn to accept his opinion, because he was wiser than we.

Any way you look at it, matings can be very frustrating. They may last three minutes of they may last over an hour. The key word is patience. One would think it was the most natural thing in the world for two dogs to mate. They do it in the streets, don't they? I can assure you that it is never that easy, but if you have your calculations right and the bitch is spot on the right day, 95 per cent of matings will result in a litter. If you are one of the 5 per cent who are unlucky, don't feel too bad, just be patient and she will probably conceive next time. We have always felt that if a bitch has missed it was meant to be. Perhaps she can gain her championship in the time between now and next season, or if she is already a champion, perhaps she will win Crufts or Westminster. There is always a reason.

Now let us assume that you have completed a successful mating and the bitch has conceived. In the early stages, you should not cosset her. She should be allowed every chance to exercise normally. There should be no change in her daily routine. Conception is not an illness. The only change I would suggest is that the bitch is introduced to the whelping box at an early stage. She will have decided by the latter stages of gestation where she intends to have the puppies. It is better if she feels at home in the whelping box long before whelping is imminent. If you introduce her to the whelping box too late, she will try to leave it and return to the place where she has decided the litter will be born, which may be under your bed if she is allowed to sleep there! The early introduction to the whelping box will alleviate this problem, thus taking much of the stress away from whelping time.

Whelping your Bitch

Let us now assume your bitch is safely in whelp as a direct consequence of satisfactory mating. It may not be totally evident whether your bitch is actually in whelp, because Rottweiler bitches tend to be very roomy and can hide a small litter up in the ribs. Many people will go to the vet and ask his opinion as to whether their bitch is in whelp or not. In the past, we have actually made this trip to the vet's and, in every case, the vet has been totally wrong. Bitches who were diagnosed in whelp consequently had no puppies, while bitches who were reported to have missed, whelped quite naturally. We therefore came to the conclusion that this course of action was a complete waste of time. Vets do now however have an extra aid to hand in cases where it is absolutely imperative to know exactly whether the bitch is or is not in whelp, in the case of bitches who, for instance, have had deliveries by Caesarean section or other problematical whelpings. The device was invented initially for testing sheep, to see whether they were having one, two or three lambs. Sheep having one lamb were put into one section, sheep having two would be put into another and sheep having three would be placed in another, because each ewe would be fed differently. The method devised was ultrasound, which has no detrimental effect on the lamb or puppy and all it does is give an ultrasonic picture, which is produced by sound only and no X-rays. This apart, I have found other methods of diagnosis so hit and miss, as to be rendered worthless.

As a rule, Rottweiler bitches, as I have said before, are not difficult whelpers. However, there is always an exception to the rule. If problems do arise, never begrudge a vet's fee. It may well save your bitch's life and possibly save your unborn litter. If your bitch has been properly exercised up to the time of whelping, she will be fit and in good condition. The extra food she has been receiving in the last two weeks prior to whelping will have all been taken by the growing whelps (*see* Chapter 5). It is a good thing to have her checked by a veterinary surgeon three of four days before she is due to whelp. He will be able to assess the condition she is in and help you with any last minute arrangements. Very few Rottweiler bitches whelp prematurely but, if this is a possibility, your vet should be able to spot this.

A couple of days before whelping, the bitch will start to look uneasy. She may even start to chew, tearing her bed up. She may rush from room to room wildly, with a worried look on her face. Bitches who whelp for the first time are usually the worst. They feel it necessary to hide their litter. They do not really want to share the experience with the owner, or any other creature. It is imperative that no strangers are allowed in the whelping area at this time, human or animal.

I know of a bitch who whelped prematurely, who had been left in a room with a companion of longstanding. Even though both the bitches were well known to each other and firm friends, the whelping bitch actually killed the puppies through anxiety. In subsequent litters, she whelped quite naturally. I have also heard of a whippet litter where the proud breeders of a first-time litter invited all their neighbours in to see the newly born puppies, who promptly filed through, coo-cooing at the newly born whelps. The bitch was put under so much stress that she licked the puppies continually, eventually licking completely through the stomach wall of two of the whelps. These actions by the bitch were brought on entirely by stress, so it is vital that the whelping area is friendly, quiet and private. It is better that only one or two members of the family visit the litter for the first week. Even then, on entering the whelping room, the first action must be to reassure the bitch, giving her a titbit, which often takes her mind off her other anxieties.

As with most quadrupeds, when she feels pain in the abdominal area, the bitch will turn her head apprehensively, looking towards her rear. She will refuse food, although in the case of many of my Rottweiler bitches of the past, they were so greedy, they would often eat their dinner completely the night before, then promptly vomit it all on the floor when they were about to whelp.

The period just before whelping is a quiet one. She will usually lie on her side, stretched out as much as possible. This is why a large whelping box is a necessity. Quietly, but breathing very deeply, in much the same way as the farrowing pig, you may hear slight grunts or whimpers at the first signs of contraction. During this period, her most favourite person can sit with her, but no one else. Even then, it would possibly be better to wait within earshot rather than to sit and stare, awaiting the first arrival.

The first arrival is the one most usually lost. This is because it arrives in a bag which is not broken by the bitch, who is either a complete novice and wonders what it is, or a bitch who has whelped before but has forgotten the routine. Consequently, the puppy drowns in the bag before the owner can get to it. Very often, the first puppy is also the largest. Once it has arrived, a veritable production line is then set into action. If the bitch shows no signs of breaking the bag, it is imperative you get in there and break it quickly with your fingers. Also, it is necessary to have a pair of sharp scissors handy to cut the umbilical cord, which we usually cut about 1in (2.5cm) away from the whelp.

TABLE SHOWING WHEN A BITCH IS DUE TO WHELP

Served Jan.	Whelps March	Served Feb.	Whelps April	Served March	Whelps May	Served April	Whelps June	Served May	Whelps July	Served June	Whelps Aug.	Served July	Whelps Sept.	Served Aug.	Whelps Oct.	Served Sept.	Whelps Nov.	Served Oct.	Whelps Dec.	Served Nov.	Whelps Jan.	Served Dec.	Whelps Feb.
1	5	1	5	1	3	1	3	1	3	1	3	1	2	1	3	1	3	1	3	1	3	1	2
2	6	2	6	2	4	2	4	2	4	2	4	2	3	2	4	2	4	2	4	2	4	2	3
3	7	3	7	3	5	3	5	3	5	3	5	3	4	3	5	3	5	3	5	3	5	3	4
4	8	4	8	4	6	4	6	4	6	4	6	4	5	4	6	4	6	4	6	4	6	4	5
5	9	5	9	5	7	5	7	5	7	5	7	5	6	5	7	5	7	5	7	5	7	5	6
6	10	6	10	6	8	6	8	6	8	6	8	6	7	6	8	6	8	6	8	6	8	6	7
7	11	7	11	7	9	7	9	7	9	7	9	7	8	7	9	7	9	7	9	7	9	7	8
8	12	8	12	8	10	8	10	8	10	8	10	8	9	8	10	8	10	8	10	8	10	8	9
9	13	9	13	9	11	9	11	9	11	9	11	9	10	9	11	9	11	9	11	9	11	9	10
10	14	10	14	10	12	10	12	10	12	10	12	10	11	10	12	10	12	10	12	10	12	10	11
11	15	11	15	11	13	11	13	11	13	11	13	11	12	11	13	11	13	11	13	11	13	11	12
12	16	12	16	12	14	12	14	12	14	12	14	12	13	12	14	12	14	12	14	12	14	12	13
13	17	13	17	13	15	13	15	13	15	13	15	13	14	13	15	13	15	13	15	13	15	13	14
14	18	14	18	14	16	14	16	14	16	14	16	14	15	14	16	14	16	14	16	14	16	14	15
15	19	15	19	15	17	15	17	15	17	15	17	15	16	15	17	15	17	15	17	15	17	15	16
16	20	16	20	16	18	16	18	16	18	16	18	16	17	16	18	16	18	16	18	16	18	16	17
17	21	17	21	17	19	17	19	17	19	17	19	17	18	17	19	17	19	17	19	17	19	17	18
18	22	18	22	18	20	18	20	18	20	18	20	18	19	18	20	18	20	18	20	18	20	18	19
19	23	19	23	19	21	19	21	19	21	19	21	19	20	19	21	19	21	19	21	19	21	19	20
20	24	20	24	20	22	20	22	20	22	20	22	20	21	20	22	20	22	20	22	20	22	20	21
21	25	21	25	21	23	21	23	21	23	21	23	21	22	21	23	21	23	21	23	21	23	21	22
22	26	22	26	22	24	22	24	22	24	22	24	22	23	22	24	22	24	22	24	22	24	22	23
23	27	23	27	23	25	23	25	23	25	23	25	23	24	23	25	23	25	23	25	23	25	23	24
24	28	24	28	24	26	24	26	24	26	24	26	24	25	24	26	24	26	24	26	24	26	24	25
25	29	25	29	25	27	25	27	25	27	25	27	25	26	25	27	25	27	25	27	25	27	25	26
26	30	26	30	26	28	26	28	26	28	26	28	26	27	26	28	26	28	26	28	26	28	26	27
27	31	27	1	27	29	27	29	27	29	27	29	27	28	27	29	27	29	27	29	27	29	27	28
28	1	28	2	28	30	28	30	28	30	28	30	28	29	28	30	28	30	28	30	28	30	28	1
29	2	29	3	29	31	29	1	29	31	29	31	29	30	29	31	29	1	29	31	29	31	29	2
30	3			30	1	30	2	30	1	30	1	30	1	30	1	30	2	30	1	30	1	30	3
31	4			31	2			31	2			31	2	31	2			31	2			31	4

190

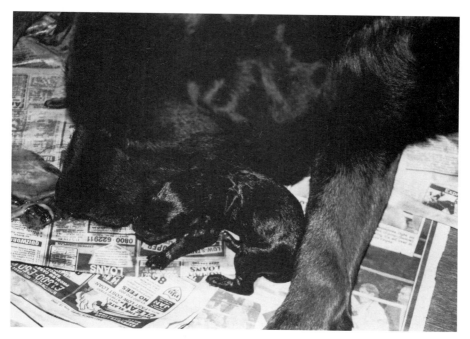

Bitch severing the umbilical cord.

These scissors must be sterilized with boiling water prior to use.

When the second whelp arrives, observe the bitch. If she is not quick to break the bag, by which I mean ten seconds, step in and break it yourself, just allowing the head outside, then pick the whelp up, complete with placenta and offer it to the bitch to finish the job herself. If she does not do this within a couple of minutes, or if another whelp starts to arrive, do it quickly yourself, repeating the process with the next puppy. It is better to teach the bitch to cope herself.

Notes should be kept on the time of arrival of each whelp. In this way, you can be absolutely clear if you need to ring the vet and tell him exactly when and where the puppies arrived. With our experience, the puppies start to arrive in the small hours of the morning in most cases. We have had morning and afternoon whelping, but they are extremely rare. Time and events become very blurred at this time of the morning, especially when you are under stress. This is why your notes are so important.

If the bitch goes a long time before having the next puppy, take her outside for a walk on the lead, just move her around. It also gives her

191

a chance to urinate or defaecate if she wants to. It would be extremely uncomfortable for her if she were not allowed to do this.

Complications

The usual presentation for birth is where the whelp is head down, head first, feet forward. Any variation from this method may need assistance. There are many ways in which you can help the bitch, but you must be totally aware of what you are doing. If the puppy becomes breeched, by which I mean, coming down back feet first, you may need to assist the bitch. If the back feet are presented, or are just slightly inside the vulva lips, you may be able to hold the back feet with a piece of cotton-wool, but I must stress you must wait for a contraction before you pull very steadily. All you are doing is keeping tension, you are not actually pulling. The whelp does not present itself at a parallel to the topline. Its presentation is almost 45 degrees to the backline. A great deal of damage can be caused to the bitch and possibly death to the whelp if it is pulled directly out. It must be pulled downwards almost as if you are making a full circle. You must only apply the gentlest of pressure, the major thrust coming from the bitch with each contraction. All you are doing is helping the whelp not to be pulled back in at the end of the contraction.

Sometimes this can happen and the bitch, with all the straining and pushing, seems to get nowhere. If you are not able to assist her, be it a breech birth or something more complicated, immediate veterinary help must be sought. You will know when this time has arrived, because the bitch will be contracting regularly, but making no progress. If this has gone on for an hour or more, it would be wise to make veterinary contact. Do not be afraid of waking the vet up. There is usually somebody who is on call for the evening. Vets are well used to calving and lambing in the early hours of the morning. It is part of their job. Before you call the vet, however, take the bitch out for one last walk of five minutes duration. Let her settle down and, if she is still in distress, call the vet.

As I have said many times, Rottweilers are particularly easy whelpers compared with many breeds. It would be unusual for you to have problems and not the general rule. When she has finished whelping, usually the next morning, call the vet anyway. He will give her an injection which will contract the uterus, pushing out all foetal debris. Also, this would flush out any remaining whelp, which is unborn. Retained whelps could be disastrous because they would merely rot

Bitch relaxing with her new-born pups.

inside the bitch, causing either death or a necessity to remove the whole of the womb by operation.

After Whelping

After whelping, the bitch should be allowed to relax and sleep. She will sleep heavily for at least two days. She should receive no solid food for twenty-four hours. We usually give just warm milk during this period and sometimes a little honey included in it for energy. It is best to leave her alone at this period and let her relax with no anxiety. However, there is one most important thing you must do and that is to ensure that all puppies do receive some colostrum, which is the first milk produced by the bitch and contains antibodies. Puppies who do not receive colostrum are far less likely to survive than those who do, and it will help to protect the puppies from infection.

Equipment Needed for Whelping

Several old towels, washed and dried. These are for vigorously rubbing the puppies once they are born and wiping nostrils clear of mucus and

193

liquid. Hold the puppy's head down and rub his back. This will usually clear the breathing tract. The puppy will still be damp when you return it to the mother; it cannot be dried completely.

One pair of curved scissors. We have found curved scissors preferential to straight ones for cutting the umbilical cord, which should be done at least 1in (2.5cm) away from the whelp.

A bowl of water containing antiseptic to rinse hands. A separate towel is also needed for this purpose.

One note pad and pen to record time of arrival. You can also weigh the puppies, but we have never found any advantage in this.

A bottle of baby oil can be used to lubricate the vulva if you find a necessity to intervene, in, say a breech birth.

Several pieces of rewashable dog bedding. The whelping box may look very smart when you first set it out, with newspaper and a piece of dog bedding on top. Even after one whelp is born, this has usually been reduced to shreds in one corner, and the newspaper totally saturated with blood and mucus. Possibly half a pint of liquid is released with each whelp. As you can imagine, a large stock of newspaper or absorbent paper needs to be held in reserve.

In northern climes, a heat lamp is also necessary. I have been told by several Germans that Rottweiler bitches have whelped outside in subzero temperatures, with no losses. This may be true, but I would suggest that this is extremely bad and irresponsible kennel management. In the natural state, the bitch would dig a hollow in which she would whelp. The puppies would be in effect under her, her heat would be retained. The hollowed shape of the nesting site would cut down on risks of puppies being squashed. I do not think a return to nature would be advisable for Rottweiler breeders of today. The German breeders who boasted of their bitch's prowess in breeding and rearing a litter in these conditions, I feel, is akin to the Spartan custom of throwing babies over the cliff if they cried. The theory that only the strong survive does not bear true, as proved by the ultimate demise of the Spartan community. I would therefore advise everyone in the northern hemisphere to make an infra-red lamp standard equipment in their whelping room. The minimum temperature I would suggest for the whelping room is around 25°C (77°F). During the first few days however, this should be slightly more increased possibly to 27/28°C (82/84°F).

It is essential that whelping and nursing bitches have plenty of water at all times. Not only is this necessary for the production of milk, but nursing bitches can become constipated. Milk does not always arrive at the same time as the whelps. Sometimes there is a little delay. If this goes on too long, however, immediate veterinary assistance must be sought.

If you have any whelps born that are either weak or small, it is possibly better to let them go. One must always judge this against the size of the litter that you have. Possibly in a very small litter, a weak puppy would be able to fight for a teat. But in a litter of eight upwards, the weaklings and the runts must be allowed to go. We have in the past spent many hours sitting up late at night nursing weakling puppies, usually to no avail. Occasionally the puppy would survive and go on to be quite a normal adult, but at this time in the history of our breed, there are too many Rottweilers around and not enough proper homes to accommodate them. It is best to concentrate on the healthy survivors. If, however, you have quite a well-grown whelp who is apparently dead, do not give up immediately. There are many cases that have been recorded where people have picked up one of these puppies, thrown it to one side, only to see the shock of its landing revive it and start its breathing. If you have a puppy that is apparently either traumatized or drowned, turn its head downwards and shake it in as rough a manner as you can, without doing it any harm. Many apparently dead puppies have been revived in this way.

Post-Whelping

For the next couple of weeks, it is essential to keep your eye on the bitch, because of possible calcium deficiency, known as eclampsia, known colloquially in farming terms as 'staggers'. The bitch will be in obvious distress, often shaking and refusing food. When she tries to rise, she will stagger, possibly fall over, as if in a drunken state. It is essential to call the vet at the first sign of there being anything wrong with your bitch. Delay will almost certainly mean death. Having said that, cases of eclampsia are extremely rare, but it is always necessary to keep an eye on the nursing bitch, for any signs of discomfort. Retained puppies or foetal debris may cause similar symptoms. Both cases can be fatal.

For the first couple of days, the bitch will sleep a great deal of the time. Puppies tend to be a little noisy during the first few days, due to the fact that milk is not coming down in any great quantity at this stage. Once milk starts to flow, happy healthy puppies will be rounded-looking and will sleep a great deal. If they are warm enough, they should sleep separately. If the whelping room however is too cold, they will huddle together to retain heat. If your puppies are gaunt-looking and long, it would be advisable to call the vet in to give them a cursory look over. Perhaps the bitch is not releasing her milk, or perhaps you have some other problem. The vet will justify his fee in this case.

By the fourth day, the puppies should be strong enough for the vet to undertake docking and removal of the rear dew-claws. Most people in the UK remove all the dew-claws. In the last couple of years, we have left front dew-claws on some litters and removed others. For my part, I think front dew-claws cause no problems and none of the litters that we have left front dew-claws on have either suffered in the working aspect or in the show ring and have certainly not been penalized for it. Some puppies have rear dew-claws, some even have double rear dew-claws. It is our policy at our kennel never to breed from or show a puppy that has had rear dew-claws.

Having carried out the docking and removal of dew-claws, this usually puts back the puppies for a couple of days. They feel generally uncomfortable until the effect has worn off. Do not worry. They will soon bounce back.

The correct way to feed a litter.

One final item, keep an eye on the puppies' nails. These usually need clipping at regular intervals. If this is not done, they form a very sharp hook, which makes the bitch's teats very sore and uncomfortable. While the puppy is sucking, he is kneading with his front paws all the time. If the teats are sore, this would be excruciatingly painful.

Weaning

We usually start weaning at about three weeks with some canned tripe covered with boiling water. The fluid from this is then poured off and cooled, forming a type of broth. Nothing is added. The pups are then introduced to the round, shallow feeding dish. To start them lapping, we gently dip their lower jaws into the broth. This will immediately start licking and searching for the food by scent and touch. It is amazing how quickly this gets them off the mark. In the past we have then generally slowly introduced larger pieces of meat. Weaning and puppy diet is discussed in greater detail in Chapter 5. All our puppies are wormed at three, five and seven weeks of age. This is extremely important. Your vet will be able to advise you on suitable worming preparations and their dosage.

9
Ailments and Diseases

Parasites

Worms

The four most common worms are *Toxocara canis*, *Toxascaris leonina* (these are two types of roundworm), *Dipylidium caninum* (a tapeworm) and *Toxoplasma gondii* (which is a protozoan parasite).

Toxocara canis This is the best known of the roundworms and since it is transmittable to man, it causes the anti-dog lobby to make hysterical outbursts every now and then. If someone could invent a way of completely destroying this horrid little beast, I do not think anyone would shed any tears at its demise. In fact, it is impossible to wipe out, because it lies dormant in the bitch until hormonal changes activate the larvae, which infect the puppies in the uterus. The puppies are born with worms already growing inside them, reaching maturity by the time the pup is only two weeks old. The larvae will burrow through the gut wall, migrating to the lungs via the liver. This causes respiratory problems. Some may be coughed up, while others pass down the digestive system, where they mature and lay thousands of eggs inside the intestine. These eggs are then passed out in the faeces to infect the soil and grass until another dog becomes host. While in the larval stage, some will lie dormant until the pup is of breedable age, when the whole thing starts again. Signs of infestation include a pot-bellied appearance with a dry staring coat.

It is important to start worming as soon as possible, because we can assume that all puppies will be infested. Worming tablets are useless on small puppies, so we use a very palatable child wormer, which we put on the puppies food in the early stages, then measured amounts are fed by syringe. Since it is extremely important that the correct dose is given, you should consult your vet for his advice. Make sure all paper from the whelping box is burned or safely disposed of, as it will inevitably be infested. Please note, the eggs are resistant to disinfectant. Do not stop worming because you do not see any worms. They may have been digested and passed out unseen in the faeces. Obviously it is not a good idea to let children play with very young puppies or nursing bitches. Eight-week-old puppies should have been wormed at least twice. Worm bitches regularly before mating.

Toxascaris leonina   This roundworm is similar in appearance to *Toxocara canis*. However, it does not migrate: the eggs simply hatch in the intestine following ingestion. They then mature in the wall of the stomach and intestine. Treatment of the infestation is the same as it is for *Toxocara canis*, with all the same precautions being taken.

Dipylidium canium   This horrid little beast is a tapeworm, and it gives me the creeps! In fact, I have only ever seen it twice, both times in the boarding kennel on longer coated dogs.

The tapeworm's body consists of segments full of eggs which are passed out in the dog's faeces. These segments look like grains of rice and are seen in the faeces and around the anus. The life cycle of the tapeworm requires an intermediate host, the flea's larva, which eats the tapeworm's eggs. When the flea reaches maturity, so does the worm larva inside it. If the dog then kills and eats the flea, as dogs do, the worm larva is released into the dog, causing infestation. Therefore action must be taken against the worm and the fleas. Your vet will advise you on what course to take.

Hookworm *(Ancylostoma caninum)*   This is a small blood-sucking worm, which can cause anaemia, sometimes severe. It is a very rare worm - I have never known of a Rottweiler infected with hookworm. However, it is only possible to diagnose it by testing faeces.

Whipworm *(Trichurius vulvis)*   Whipworm eggs live in the soil and are very resilient. It is a very small worm and diagnosis is made in the same way as with hookworm. Consult your vet for faeces testing and treatment. It is very unlikely you will come across hookworm or whipworm in Rottweilers.

Toxoplasma gondii   This parasite is found in cats. However, it will use dogs or humans as intermediary hosts. Dogs can pick up the parasite's eggs from cat's faeces and also from infected raw meat. (Cooking kills the parasite.) If eaten by a dog, the eggs come to maturity and attack the tissues forming cysts in the muscles and sometimes in the brain. These then lie dormant, only to be released in times of stress or ill health. Clinical signs are rare, because attacks on dogs are usually very mild. Again, attacks can only be diagnosed by a veterinarian. Make sure your dog has no access to cat droppings or uncooked meat which could be infected.

Lungworm *(Filaroides osleri)* Infection largely goes unnoticed, but the first indication is a harsh dry cough and loss of condition. Mature worms are to be found in the nodules on the trachea and bronchi. Treatment is very difficult and may need surgery. However, it is an extremely rare worm.

Heart worm These worms are spread by mosquito and so need not worry people in the northern hemisphere. A dog is bitten by the mosquito, which deposits the worm larvae, which will then burrow into a vein. They are transported via the bloodstream to the heart, where they live until finally killing their host by causing heart failure by means of blocking the flow of blood.

With all worm infestations, or where puppies are whelped in the house, you must be aware that young children can pick up eggs, which might cause illness. Pet dogs can be wormed regularly and a sample of faeces taken to the veterinary surgeon once a year to test for infection. A small infestation will be tolerated by the dog with no obvious outward sign of illness, so a regular test is the only way to be sure.

Fleas

The life cycle of the flea starts with the egg being laid in the sleeping quarters of the dog, which could be your carpet or the dog's favourite chair. They hatch between two and fifteen days into the larval stage. In one or two weeks, they develop to mature pupae. The adult flea hatches from the pupa at variable times, largely depending on the temperature.

I once saw a rabbit shot and it was quite amazing to see the reaction of the flea population, who immediately migrated to the ears of the dead host. I cannot help feeling that if the dog had picked up the rabbit, he would have inherited this large colony as his own.

The movement of the flea causes irritation to the dog, who will bite himself in a preening action. The owner observing this behaviour should check for signs of fleas. Flea droppings are the most obvious sign: they are black or red and look like sand in the coat. If you comb out the coat and put some of the grains on paper and wet them, they will stain red.

Fleas can cause many skin problems and, as mentioned before, the flea acts as a host for the tapeworm larvae. They should be destroyed with insecticidal shampoo or sprays which are obtainable from your vet or from good pet shops but it is important that treatment is repeated, according to the manufacturer's instructions, especially if infestation is acute. It is also vital to treat the dog's environment – his bed or kennel, your carpets and upholstery – since most of the flea's life cycle, including its egg laying, is spent away from its host.

Lice

Lice spend their life cycle on the host. They feed on the skin and lay eggs on the hair. Modern insecticides prepared for the purpose are effective at destroying lice but treatment should be repeated to ensure complete eradication. Unlike fleas, lice cannot survive for long away from the dog, so treatment of the environment is not necessary.

Ticks

Dogs can pick up ticks from blades of grass and hedges in areas frequented by sheep, the tick's natural host. They should be removed by applying surgical spirit or ether to loosen the tick's mouthparts, which are embedded in the dog's skin. Having loosened its hold it can be removed with tweezers. It is vital that the tick is removed with its head intact, otherwise local infection may result. If in any doubt, you should consult your vet who will safely remove the tick for you.

Appendix 1

Glossary of German Terms

Abzeichen (A)   markings
Ahnentafel   pedigree
Allgemeine Erscheinung
   general appearance
Alter   age
Angekört   certified suitable for
   breeding
Aufmerksam   attentive
Augen   eyes
Ausdruck   character
Ausreichend (A)   satisfactory
Bauch   belly
Befriedigend (B)   fair
Behaarung   coat
Belegt   bred
Besitzer   owner
Bewegung   movement
Brand   markings
Braun   brown
Breit   broad
Brust (Br)   chest
Dunkel (D)   dark
Ehrenpreis   Prize of Honour
Ellenbogen   elbow
Eltern   parents
Eng   narrow
Erziehung   upbringing
Farbe   colour
Fassbeine   bow-legged
Fassrippe   barrel-ribbed
Flanke   loin
Flott   stylish, smart

Fluchtig   fleet
Flussig   fluid (movement)
Fröhlich   happy
Gang   gait
Ganz   complete
Gelb (G)   gold
Geschleschtsgeprage   sex-
   quality
Gesundheit   sound health
Gewinkelt   angulated
Geworfen   whelped
Glatterhaarig   smooth-coated
Greifbar   tangible
Gross   large
Grosseltern   grandparents
Gut (G)   good
Hals   throat, neck
Harmonisch   co-ordinated
Hart   hardness
Hasenfuss   hare-foot(ed)
Hinterbeine   hind legs
Hocke   hock
Hoden   testicles
Hohe   height
Hund   dog (applies to male
and female)
Hundin (H)   bitch
Jugend   youth
Jugendklasse (JK)   youth class
Junghund   puppy
Kampf   struggle
Katzenfus   catfoot

Allgemeiner Deutscher Rottweiler-Klub e. V.	Katalog-Nr.:
Richterbericht	119

		ZB-Nr.:	Wurftag:
Name: Eika vom Barrenstein	R☐ H☒ 65 239		27.01.85
Besitzer: F. Schnorr, 5439 Bellingen	HD: 0		AKz.:

Gesamteindruck: mittelgroß, in guter Substanz i. passender Knochenstärke, insges. jugendl. weich(Schulter,

Wesen: ruhig, aufmerksam   Ellenbogen, Rücken)

Beurteilung: Brand gut i. d. Farbe u. Verteilung, Augen dunkelbraun m. gutem Schnitt, Ohren in passender Form, werden gut getragen, starke Lefzen mit insges. guter Pigmentierung, in den Ellenbogen noch wenig straff, Vorhand gerade, kräftige Pfoten, gute Rücken-linie, gute Winkelung der Hinterhand, im Lauf flüssig u. etwas hakeneng, gutes Gebiß.

BEWERTUNG:

sg 1

☐ Gebr.-H.-Klasse
☐ Offene Klasse
☐ Junghundklasse
☒ Jugendklasse
☐ Jüngstenklasse
☐ Veteranenklasse

Ort: Pfungstadt

Datum: 13.04.1986

W. Feupres

Unterschrift

Critique on the author's dog from a German show.

Kippohr soft ear		**Oberarm** upper arm	
Klein small		**Oberschlachtig** overshot	
Knocken bones		**Ohr** ear	
Kraft power		**Pfote** paw	
Kräftig strong		**Rasse** breed	
Kragen collar		**Raum** space	
Kruppe croup		**Rippen** ribs	
Kurz short		**Richtig** correct	
Lang long		**Rücken** back	
Länge length		**Rude (R)** dog	
Lauf run		**Rute** tail	
Mangelhaft (M) poor		**Schädel** skull	
Muskeln muscles		**Scherengebib** scissor bite	
Mutter dam		**Scheu** shy	
Nachschub drive, thrust		**Schöner** beautiful	
Nagel claw		**Schönheit** beauty	
Nase nose		**Schulter** shoulder	

Allgemeiner Deutscher Rottweiler-Klub (ADRK) e.V., Sitz Stuttgart

Zuchttauglichkeitsprüfungsbericht

Ort: Grefrath
Tag: 14.3.1987
Körmeister/Richter: Apel Gerhard

für den Rüden / die Hündin: Anuschka von Alt-Mengenich Wurftag: 21.6.1985

ZB-Nr.: 66267 SchH: HD: – HD-Register-Nr.: 9311

Vater: Attila von der Kölner-Bucht ZB-Nr.: 55330

Mutter: Alfa von Haus Gronemann ZB-Nr.: 61774

Züchter: Willi Renter,

Besitzer: Th. u. K. Kölkes, Bruckhauserstr. 22, 4155 Grefrath

Mitglieds-Nr.: 0700330

Körpermaße

Widerristhöhe: 58 cm, Brusttiefe: 28 cm, Gewicht: 38 kg
Rumpflänge: 70 cm, Brustumpfang: 79 cm,
Oberkopf: 9 14 cm, Fang: 14 9 cm,

Erscheinung und Verfassung, Gebäude und Ganganlagen:

mittelgroß, sehr gutim Typ liegend, mit passender Knochenstärke,
sehr schöner typischer Kopf, Ohren mittelgroß, korrekt getragen, Augen
braun, Pigmentierung der Zahnleisten leicht rosa, Lefzen dunkel, kräftiger
Hals, Oberarm noch etwas lose, Vorhand korrekt, Pfoten kräftig, Brust
von guter Breite und Tiefe, sehr gute Nacken- und Rückenlinie, kräftiges
Stockhaar, mit sichtbarer Unterwolle am Hals, Hinterhand sehr gut ge-
stellt und gewinkelt, natürliche Ganganlagen, Scherengebiß.

Wesen:

	gering	mittel	hoch	sehr hoch		gering	mittel	hoch	sehr hoch
Selbstsicherheit			X		Unerschrockenheit			X	
Temperament			X		Aufmerksamkeit			X	
Führigkeit		X			Mißtrauen			X	
Mut			X		Kampftrieb			X	
Schutztrieb			X		Härte			X	
Reizschwelle		X							

	gleichgültig	leicht	scheu
Reaktion auf den Schuß	X		

	zuchttauglich	zurückgestellt	zuchtuntauglich
Vorführung: 1	Richterurteil:	X		

Bestätigung der Zuchtbuchstelle
Vorstehendes Ergebnis ist für den Hund eingetragen
Porta Westfalica 4, den 30. April 1987

Körmeister/Richter: _____ Unterschrift

Hauptzuchtwart: _____ Unterschrift

ZTP breed assessment certificate issued by ADRK. 'X' should fall in the shaded areas for best marks.

204

Schulterblatt shoulder blade
Schuss-scheu gun-shy
Schussfest gun-proof
Schwanz tail
Schwarz black
Sehr gut (SG) very good
Stell steep
Stockhaar harsh coat
Temperamentvoll
  temperament complete
Tief deep
Traben trotting
Trocken dry
Uberwinkelt over-angulated
Ungenügend (U) unsatisfactory

Unterschlachtig undershot
Vater sire
Verteilung allotment
Vorderbeine forelegs
Vorderbrust forechest
Vorschub reach
Vorzüglich excellent
Weich soft
Weise manner, way
Weiss white
Werfen whelped
Wesen temperament
Wesenscheu shyness
Widerrist withers

Glossary of Abbreviations

Hip Dysplasia Degrees

HD- Normal hips (*Korfähig*)
HD+/- Minor changes (*Korfähig*)
HD+ Hip dysplasia present but mild. Breeding is restricted to certain partners and dogs with this grading are not eligible for the *Korung Zuchttauglich*.
HD++ Hip dysplasia present. Breeding forbidden. (*Zuchtverbot*.)
HD+++ Hip dysplasia severe. Breeding forbidden. (*Zuchtverbot*.)

Working Degrees (Schutzhundprüfung)

SchH. Schutzhund. (Protection dog.) The most common training degree on German pedigrees. This protection phase is only one third of the total test, which also includes tracking and obedience. To be awarded SchH I, II or III, a dog must score a pass mark in each of the phases and gain a total of at least 220 points out of a possible 300.
IPO *Internationale Prüfungsordnung*. (International Examination.) An international test similar to Schutzhund, awarded by the FCI. It also comes in three degrees: I, II and III.
FH *Fahrtenhund*. (Tracking degree.)

205

AD   *Ausdauer Prüfung*. (Endurance Test.) Dogs offering for the *Korung* must pass this test.

BLH   *Blindenhund*. (Guide Dog for the Blind.)

DH   *Diensthund*. (Service Dog.)

MIL DH   *Militardiensthund*. (Military Service Dog Degree.)

PH   *Polizeihund*. (Police Dog.)

PSP   *Polizeischutzhundprüfung*.   (Police Protection Dog.)

ZH   *Zollhund*. (Customs Dog.)

Appendix 2

German Working Champions

1949	(München)	Pluto v Jakobsbrunnen
1950	(München)	Kleine Siegerprufung
1951	(Dortmund)	Blanca v Cilabrunnen
1952	(Nurnberg)	Marko v Filstalstrand
1953	(Bremen)	Barry v Rheintor
1954	(Niefern)	Der Titel 'Leistungsseiger' wurde nicht vergenben
1955	(Frankfurt)	Barry v Rheintor
1956	(Frankfurt)	Kleine Siegerprüfung
1957	(Düsseldorf)	Castor v d Bokermuhle
1958	(Stuttgart)	Arko v Hipplerhof
1959	(Obërhausen)	Axel v Spiekerhof
1960	(Niefern)	Bob v Hause Hader
1961	(Nurnberg)	Arko v Fichtenschlag
1962	(Nurnberg)	Kleine Siegerprüfung
1963	(Ober-Castrop)	Dolf v d Schmechting
1964	(Idar-Oberstein)	Arras v Moritzberg
1965	(Bayreuth)	Droll v Baumbusch
1966	(Stüttgart)	Quick v d Solitude
1967	(Obërhausen)	Ajax v Asenberg
1968	(Heppenheim)	Casar v.d Luneburger Heide
1969	(Nurnberg)	Alc Zerberus
1970	(Hannover)	Armin v Konigshardt
1971	(Castrop-Rauxel)	Armin v Konigshardt
1972	(Aalen)	Axel v d Wegscheide
1973	(Troisdorf-Spich)	Cralo v Mischa
1974	(Ilvesheim)	Felix v Sonnenberg
1975	(Obërhausen)	Astor v Hause Pfarr
1976	(Bayreuth)	Barry v Waldhuck
1977	(Neuwied)	Barry v Waldhuck
1978	(Goslar)	Etzel v Amselhof
1979	(Blatzheim)	Osko v Klosterchen

1980	(Idar-Obërstein)	Axel v Rhein-Elbe-Park
1981	(Gladbeck)	Bengo v Klosterchen
1982	(Stadhagen)	Axel v Rhein-Elbe-Park
1983	(Trossingen)	Axel v Rhein-Elbe-Park
1984	(Oeding)	Enzor v Saufang
1985	(Rehburg)	Erasmus v Magdeberg
1986	(Konigsbach)	Casar v d Wester Lohe
1987	(Herten)	Rocco v Horster Dreieck
1988	(Oeding)	Max v Konigsgarten
1989	(Asheberg-Herbern)	Rocco v Horster Dreieck

Klubsiegers

1971	KSZ in Rottweil	Bulli v Hungerbuhl
1972	KSZ in Köln	Bulli v Hungerbuhl
1973	KSZ in Porta Westfalica	Greif v Fleischer
1974	KSZ in Rottweil	Karol v Wellesweiler
1975	KSZ in Niefern-Oschelbronn	Axel v Fusse der Eifel
1976	KSZ in Aachen	Ari v Walduck
1977	KSZ in Niefern-Oschelbronn	Carlo v Fusse der Eifel
1978	KSZ in Borken-Burlo	Alas
1979	KSZ in Rottweil	Condor zur Klamm
1980	KSZ in Bad Eilsen	Dingo v Schwaiger Wappen
1981	KSZ in Bensheim/Bergstrabe	Nero v Schloss Rietheim
1982	KSZ in Stadthagen	Bronco v Rauberfeld
1983	KSZ in Blatzheim	Mirko v Steinkopf
1984	KSZ in Niefern	Falko v d Tente
1985	KSZ in Coesfeld	Hassan v Konigsgarten
1986	KSZ in Ilvesheim	Iwan v Fusse der Eifel
1987	KSZ in Ascheberg-Herbern	Ilco v Fusse der Eifel
1988	KSZ in Rottweil	Gary v Gruntenblick
1989	KSZ in Herten	Danjo v Schwaiger Wappen

Klubsiegerinnen

1971	KSZ in Rottweil	Dolli v d Meierei
1972	KSZ in Köln	Edda v Schloss Ickern
1973	KSZ in Porta Westfalicia	Afra v Haus Schottroy
1974	KSZ in Rottweil	Anka v Lohauserholz

1975	KSZ in Niefern-Oschlerbronn	Biene v Geiselstein
1976	KSZ in Aachen	Asta v Lohauserholz
1977	KSZ in Niefern-Oschelbronn	Asta v Lohauserholz
1978	KSZ in Borken-Burlo	Assy v Haugenfeld
1979	KSZ in Rottweil	Assy v Haugenfeld
1980	KSZ in Bad Eilsen	Babette v Magdeberg
1981	KSZ in Bensheim/Bergstrasse	Carmen v Old Germany
1982	KSZ in Stadthagen	Itta v Zimmerplatz
1983	KSZ in Blatzheim	Hulda v Konigsgarten
1984	KSZ in Niefern	Hulda v Konigsgarten
1985	KSZ in Coesfeld	Yvonne v Markgraferland
1986	KSZ in Ilvesheim	Anka v d Nonnenhohle
1987	KSZ in Ascheberg-Herbern	Golda v Sonnenberg
1988	KSZ in Rottweil	Cita v d Nonnenhohle
1989	KSZ in Herten	Ina v d Silberdistel

Appendix 3

List of Current EzA Certificate Holders
(Breeding Lifetime Certificate)

Points	Name	ZB-#
290	Ambassador v Freienfels	60 288
284	Beppo v Godewind	63 709
283	Gabriel v Dengelberg	57 900
280	I L C O v Fusseder Eifel	62 647
279	Django v Heltorfer Forst	57 005
276	Iwan v Fusseder Eifel	62 651
276	Morris v Rauchfang	60 326
276	Bulli v Bayernland	58 896
273	Baas v d Siegbrücke	64 111
273	Alex v Südharz	59 012
272	Orpheus v Schwaiger Wappen	59 462
271	Endo v Leinetal	62 964
270	Mirko v Hohenhameln	58 592
269	Maro v Rauchfang	60 326
265	Aki v d Peeler Hütte	63 168
263	Max v Duracher Tobel	61 556
253	Brando v d Aar Mundung	59 055
250	Benno v Florian	61 430
240	Aki v Barrenstein	61 329
234	Blitz v Hause Gronemann	63 716

Appendix 4

South African Kennel Union Regulations for Dog Carting
(Schedule, 5(G))

1 Licensing and Show Regulations

The regulations and other matters to do with shows as set out in Schedule 3, Regulations for Championship Shows (Breed) and Schedule 4, Regulations for Non-Championship Shows (Breed), of the Kennel Union of South Africa shall apply to dog carting in so far as they do not conflict with the specific terms of this Schedule 5(G).

2 Scope of the Licence

2.1 A club which is qualified to hold a Championship Show may hold a Championship and/or Non-Championship Dog Carting Event in conjunction with either of such shows under the same licence or separate licence.

2.2 A club which is not qualified to hold a Championship Show may hold a Non-Championship Dog Carting Event in conjunction with such event and under the same licence or separate therefrom.

3 Eligibility for Competition

Any dog may compete which is registered with the Kennel Union of Southern Africa in the Breed Register, Obedience and Working Trials Record or in the Development Register and it is not in conflict with the regulations hereunder described or who has not been disqualified or suspended from competition by the Kennel Union of Southern Africa.

4 Carting Certificates

4.1 A KUSA Carting Certificate will be awarded at any Championship Show to any dog that gains at least 95 per cent of the marks awardable in the Senior Class.

Mrs Barbara Butler with Ch. Upend Gallant Theodoric and friend.

4.2   A qualifying Carting Certificate will be awarded at any Championship Show to any dog that gains at least 90 per cent of the marks in the Novice Class.

4.3   Champion Status: a dog awarded 3 KUSA Carting Certificates, each by a different judge, will qualify as a Carting Champion and a KUSA Certificate to this effect will be issued.

5 Registering and Eligibility of Dogs for Competition

5.1   Only those dogs which are entered in the Breed Register, Development Register or the Obedience and Trial Dogs Record may compete in any carting event.

5.2   No dog may compete in a higher grade until it has received two (2) qualifying Carting Certificates in the Novice Class.

5.3   A dog having become eligible to compete in a class may continue to compete in that class until it is suspended or disqualified from competition, or until it has qualified in the higher class.

5.4   It is permissible to enter a dog for competition in a carting event in anticipation of the dog qualifying to compete in that event at a previous show, provided that the entry is made in accordance with the rules of the club holding the carting event and that the dog qualifies prior to the day of the show.

6 Qualification of Judges

6.1   No person may judge at a carting event until he has attended a carting judges training course.

6.2   No person may judge at a Championship Carting Event unless he has submitted reports on two (2) Non-Championship Carting Events and those reports have been approved by the Provincial Council in the area in which he has judged.

6.3   In order to be placed on the panel of Carting Judges, the judge must judge two (2) Championship Carting Events and reports on those must be approved by the Federal Council.

6.4   No report by a judge will be considered, which does not contain a detailed comment on the performance of the first two and the last dog placed in the class.

6.5   Appointments of judges normally resident outside the area of jurisdiction of the KUSA will be considered by the Federal Council in the light of the judge's qualifications recognized by the appropriate canine authority in the judge's country of residence.

6.6   Until such time as there are sufficient judges qualified to judge a carting event, any person who has attended a carting judges training course and is in possession of a licence to judge Class A Obedience or a higher class will be automatically qualified to judge a Championship Carting Event.

7 Management of Carting Events

7.1   Carting Show Manager. The management of a carting show shall be entrusted to the carting show manager who shall be appointed by the committee of the club holding the Show.

7.2   Disputes. Any disputed matter requiring a decision of the ground shall be decided by the carting show manager and the judge(s). However, the control of all matters connected with the dogs during competition shall rest with the judge(s) of the event, but the manager, if required, may be called upon for assistance.

7.3   Complaints. Complaints lodged by competitors will be dealt with in accordance with the KUSA Regulations.

7.4   Other Matters. Any matter not provided for in the KUSA Regulations for carting events shall be decided by a majority of the carting show manager and the judge(s) at the show and their decision shall be final. In the event of a majority not being obtained, the KUSA Representative shall appoint a referee to make a majority.

7.5 Misbehaviour of Dogs at a Show.

7.5.1 Physical disciplining of a dog or serious uncontrollable behaviour of a dog at a carting event may be penalized at the discretion of the carting show manager by excluding the dog and/or handler from further competition at the show and/or by ordering the exhibitor of the dog to forfeit any carting awards, positions or qualifications gained at the Show.

7.5.2 Should the behaviour of any handler or dog threaten the safety or well-being of the dog and/or the safety or well-being of the handler and/or some other dog or person and/or any physical property, then in such an event, neither the handler nor the dog shall be permitted to complete any exercises being carried out on that day and shall be reported to the Show Secretary, who will render a written report to the Federal Council detailing the circumstances.

7.6 Number of Dogs to be Judged. No judge shall be required to test more than a total of twenty (20) dogs in one day. When the number of entries to be judged by one person exceeds these limits, the committee of the club holding the show shall appoint an extra judge(s) and shall allocate competitors as equally as possible among the judges by draw.

7.7 Handler of Dog. Either the owner or deputy may handle the dog, but it must be one or the other. Once the dogs have commenced work, an owner must not interfere with his dog if he has deputed another person to handle it.

7.8 Competing Dogs. No bitch in season shall be allowed to compete in any carting event. Spayed bitches and castrated dogs may compete.

7.9 Conditions. It is the responsibility of the carting event manager and of the judge(s) to ensure that all dogs competing in an event compete under the same conditions as far as this is practical.

7.10 Weather. It shall be at the sole discretion of the judge whether or not competition in any event should be interrupted on account of inclement weather. Cancellation of a carting event or of any part of a carting event shall be at the discretion of the carting event show manager in consultation with the judge(s).

7.11 Starting Time. All competitors shall be informed of the starting time for their event and competitors and dogs in each event shall be present at the site of the Show at least thirty (30) minutes before that time. The judge shall have discretion to postpone the starting time of an event, and the draw or order of competition, for a reasonable period if competitors in the event are delayed through competition elsewhere in the show falling behind schedule and such postponement shall be made known to all competitors in the event who are present. Any competitor who is not present at the end of such postponement shall be regarded as withdrawn from the show and shall not be allowed to compete.

7.12 Order of Competition. The order of competition shall be determined by draw among the competitors in each event, immediately before the first exercise of the event is due to begin.

7.13 The carting event manager is responsible for the demarcation of the areas to be used for carting events and is responsible for ensuring that the areas comply with these Regulations. The show-holding club shall be responsible for supplying all the necessary equipment.

7.14 Competition by Officials at Shows. No judge at a show or the KUSA Representative may enter or handle a dog for competition in any section at that show (Breed, Obedience, Working Trial or Carting Event) on any day on which he is officiating.

7.15 Catalogue Numbers. Handlers must display catalogue numbers prominently when in the ring.

7.16 The suggested size of the working area or ring should be 30 metres by 30 metres.

Schedule of Exercises – Carting Work Exercises

1.   **Novice Class** All work done on lead.
1.1   Basic control
1.1.1   Heel work (10 points)
1.1.2   Recall (10 points)
1.1.3   Stay - a group exercise (10 points)
1.2   Harnessing and hitching (10 points)
1.3   Basic commands (15 points)
1.4   Manoeuvring (35 points)
1.4.1   Control in the presence of a distraction (10 points)
2.   **Senior Class** All work done off lead.
2.1   Basic control
2.1.1   Heel work (10 points)
2.1.2   Recall (10 points)
2.1.3   Stay – a group exercise (10 points)
2.2   Harnessing and hitching (10 points)
2.3   Basic commands (15 points)
2.4   Manoeuvring (35 points)

2.4.1   Control in the presence of a distraction (10 points)

3.   **Description of Exercises**

3.1   Heel work. The handler will present himself at the place indicated by the judge with his dog on lead in the heel position (i.e. sitting at heel at the handler's working side). From the start of the exercise, the handler will move with his dog as directed by the judge. The object of the exercise is to test the dog's ability to remain naturally at the handler's working side while moving at normal, fast and slow paces. The exercise will include right turns, left turns, about turns and halts.

3.2.   Recall. Upon order from the judge, the handler will leave his dog in the sit/down posture (at handler's choice) and move forward at judge's discretion for a distance of approximately 20 metres, when he will halt and about turn to face his dog. On order from the judge, the handler will call his dog which must come smartly to the handler, to sit straight in front of him. On order from the judge, the handler will command his dog to heel position. In the Senior Class, the exercise can be varied (at the discretion of the judge), by having the dog recalled while the handler is on the move away from the dog. The dog is to move smartly to the working side of the handler and is to continue forward in the heel position until the halt command is given.

3.3   **Stay (a group exercise).**

   3.3.1   Novice Class - one minute down-stay. The dogs are to remain in the down posture. The handler will move forward in a direction as commanded by the judge and halt on command. After the time has elapsed, the handlers will return to their dogs on command by the judge. A dog shall not be penalized for reasonable movement provided it does not move from the required posture (down) or move more than its own body length form its position.

   3.3.2   Senior Class - Three minute stay. As for the Novice Class, except at the judge's discretion, the dog shall be left in any one of the three postures (down, sit, stand) for a period of three minutes. Handlers can be requested to move out of sight of the dogs, at the judge's discretion.

3.4   **Harnessing and Hitching**.

   3.4.1   Prior to the exercise, the handler places the harness in the cart and positions the cart as indicated by the judge.

   3.4.2   At the command of the judge, the handler and dog enter the ring to a position as indicated by the judge. The handler leaves the dog in the stay position, fetches the harness and returns to the dog. The dog remains in the stay position and obeys commands for harnessing by the handler. The dog and handler walk to the cart, where the dog stands or backs up for hitching. The handler indicates his readiness and awaits the judge's examination for the harnessing and hitching.

3.5 Basic Commands. With the cart now hitched and under the direction of the judge, the dog will perform the following exercises: haul forward at normal pace; fast pace; slow pace; stop (stand/sit); back up and stay.

3.6 Manoeuvring. The course will be completed by the handler and dog pulling its cart.

Novice Class – At the direction of the judge.

Senior Class – Either at the direction of the judge or without the judge's instructions (at the discretion of the judge).

3.6.1   The cart should be loaded with a load provided by the judge, according to the size of the dog. The placing and securing of the load should cause no discomfort to the dog.

3.6.2   The course to be followed by the handler and dog shall include all the following: circular patterns; at least three (3) turns of 90 degrees, two of which shall be in a different direction; broad curves; narrow areas; removable obstacles (a gate, branch or similar).

Rottweiler fun day in aid of charity, 1990.

3.6.3   The back up should be performed during the manoeuvring course. The purpose of the back up is to show that the harnessed dog, should the handler inadvertently lead him into a tight corner where turning is impossible, is able to back up on command. To this end, an alley is created simulating a dead-end and which is wide enough to allow the dog with cart and handler in. Then, by means of hand signals and commands, the handler instructs the dog to back up a distance, at least equal to the length of the dog and cart, until he has reversed out of the dead-end.

3.6.4   At a point to be determined by the judge, a distraction is created. The distraction should not occur at a point where a basic command is given or to be given. Allowable is a short stop, a prolonged stare, or a short bark. No deviation either toward or away from the distraction is permitted.

4.   Handling of Dogs

4.6.1   Should a handler touch his dog whilst such dog is completing any exercise, points will be deducted each time this is necessary.

4.6.2   In the Novice Class, handlers may encourage and talk to their dogs whilst competing in an exercise and may guide their dogs into position between exercises.

4.6.3   Pats and physical praise are allowed and encouraged at the completion of the whole course.

4.6.4   Any dog which, during any exercise, leaves the ring, upsets the cart or shows aggressive tendencies, will fail that exercise unless the judge, using his discretion as to the circumstances, permits the dog to continue.

4.6.5   If any dog is not under control at any time during the course of the exercises, that dog will be excluded from that exercise.

Appendix 5

Breed Clubs

United Kingdom

The Northern Rottweiler Club
     Mr Anderson
     17 Larun Beat
     Yarn
     Cleveland

The Eastern Counties Rottweiler Club
     Mrs K. Hindley
     1 Hard Lane
     Kiveton Park
     Sheffield
     South Yorkshire

The Northern Ireland Rottweiler Club
     Mr W. McCullum
     3 Highdene Gardens
     Belfast
     Northern Ireland

The British Rottweiler Association
     Mrs M. Hayward
     35 Hoe Lane
     Enfield
     Middlesex

The Rottweiler Club
     Miss E. Harrap
     Pangorra
     Grays Pond
     Goring Heath
     Reading
     Berkshire

LASER
    The Methodist Church Hall
    Jeffreys Road
    Stockwell
    London

The Midlands Rottweiler Club
    Mrs J. Heath
    97 Upper Meadow Road
    Quinton
    Birmingham
    West Midlands

The Rottweiler Welfare Association
    Mrs C. Tate
    3 Vernon Avenue
    Peacehaven
    Sussex

Australia

The Rottweiler Club of Victoria
    Mrs Helen Read
    57 Copparos Road
    Newcomb 3219
    Victoria

The Rottweiler Club of Queensland
    Brisbane City Soccer Club
    Spencer Park
    Newberry Street
    Newmarket
    Brisbane
    Queensland

New Zealand

Central Rottweiler Club of New Zealand
    Linda Wisnesky
    6 Frethey Crescent
    Naenae

South Africa

Meridian Rottweiler Club
        Mr D. Lower
        Box 1938
        Halfway House
        Transvaal

Germany

Allgemeiner Deutscher Rottweiler Klub (ADRK)
        Rintelner Strasse 385
        4952 Portia Westfa

United States

Jolain Engel
        10 800 S W
        67 Court Miami
        Florida 33457

Jamaica

Rottweiler Club of Jamaica
        Winston Tucker
        P O Box 352
        Kingston 11

Norway

Norsk Rottweiler Klubb
        Tenja Johansen
        Postboks 6732
        St Olavsplass
        Oslo 1

Bibliography

Burns, Marca and Fraser, Margaret *Genetics of the Dog*, Oliver & Boyd (First ed. 1952, reprinted 1966)

Chardet, D. *Ken Un Rottweiler*, Elsevier, Amsterdam/Brussels (1977)

Evans, J.M. and White, Kay *Doglopaedia*, Henston (1987)

Fleig, Dr D. *Kampfhunde II*, H Bohm, H Prell & H Weber (1983)

Fox, M.W. *Understanding Your Dog*, Blond & Briggs (1974)

Hall, Patricia *The Rottweiler in Australia*

Hubbard C.L.B. *Dogs in Britain*, Macmillan, London (1948)

Koehler, *The Koehler Method of Guard Dog Training*, Howell Book House Inc., New York (1967)

Lyons, McDowell *The Dog In Action*, Howell Book House Inc., New York (1985)

Mulvany, Mollie *All About Obedience Training for Dogs*, Pelham Books, London (1986)

Portman Graham, Capt. R. *The Mating and Whelping of Dogs*, Popular Dogs, London (1986)

Spooner, Glenda *The Handbook of Showing*, London Museum Press Ltd., London (1977)

Yrjola, J. A. U. and Tikka, Elvi *Our Friend the Rottweiler*, Powderhorn Press (1982)

Index